Methodology of Progressive
SOCIAL WORK EDUCATION

Sourcebook Series on Social Work Education
Tata Institute of Social Sciences

Methodology of Progressive SOCIAL WORK EDUCATION

Murli Desai

RAWAT PUBLICATIONS
Jaipur • New Delhi • Bangalore • Hyderabad • Guwahati

ISBN 81-7033-889-1

Reprinted, 2011

Published by
Prem Rawat for **Rawat Publications**
Satyam Apts., Sector 3, Jawahar Nagar, Jaipur - 302 004 (India)
Phone: 0141 265 1748 / 7006 Fax: 0141 265 1748
E-mail : info@rawatbooks.com
Website: rawatbooks.com

New Delhi Office
4858/24, Ansari Road, Daryaganj, New Delhi 110 002
Phone: 011-23263290

Also at *Bangalore, Hyderabad* and *Guwahati*

Typeset by Rawat Computers, Jaipur
Printed at Nice Printing Press, New Delhi

Contents

Foreword

The Sourcebook on *Methodology of Progressive Social Work Education* constitutes a part of a path-breaking Sourcebook Series on Social Work Education planned by the Social Work Education and Practice Cell of the Tata Institute of Social Sciences, Mumbai. After conducting the UGC-sponsored refresher courses for social work educators for more than 15 years, such a contribution is indeed timely and will be further useful for such training programmes as well as self-assessment, self-development and capacity-building of institutions for social work education. Different chapters of this volume, namely, building a perspective, curriculum development, teaching-learning and evaluation, training and knowledge development, dissemination and retrieval for progressive social work education, provide the reader a rich treat from perspective to practice.

The institutions for social work education are at different levels of development and are also working in different contexts. Based on the methodology recommended in this book, users can reflect, create, initiate and adopt their own applications rather than repeat or reproduce the application demonstrated mechanically. Any user will find in it ideas which can facilitate change from a *wish list* to a creative *work list* through proper perception of changing reality with competence and confidence.

In any curriculum of social work (basic or foundation courses, optional courses and specialization courses), there is a need to examine the relationship and relevance of each course as well as between different courses, and further relate them with the semester-wise *course for field practice*. But, except for one, no institution of social work has devised a curriculum of field practice, and the application of course work to fieldwork is more assumed than real. It is the latter, which informs, socializes, liberates and integrates. The need for accountability is therefore uppermost in this area. In the school of social work where the curriculum of fieldwork has been drafted, there has been no feedback so far on its operationalisation and impact. So is the case with the field action projects of various institutions of social work. The periodic input-output exercises are yet to be conducted in order to improve professional investment-in-practice. Formal discourses on adult learners, human rights, gender, or entitlement perspectives, theories of learning and types of students (that is, compliant, anxious, dependent, independent, attention-seeking, silent and ignorable) are not enough. These demand professional intervention, for the types of students are products-in-process, and manifestations of the self at a point of time or over time. Participatory research or practice can strengthen such professional intervention and its components. People, power and praxis, which are central to it, are again the manifestations of the collective self in that one needs to know how these are situated, distributed and acted upon and how social work can facilitate their interaction and enhancement.

At the ideational level, this Sourcebook has been under preparation for more than a decade and it has been enriched by the convergence of several roles that Professor Murli Desai played during this period first as the Head of Unit for Family Studies and Associate Editor of *The Indian Journal of Social Work* and now as the Head, Social Work Education and Practice Cell at the Tata Institute of Social Sciences. Her readings, reflections and interactions during this period are evident in the domains of knowledge, attitude and practice of the methodology of progressive social work education. It is hoped that more social work educators will come forward to document and disseminate their experiences and thereby contribute to different aspects of professional education as humble 'servant-leaders'. I congratulate Professor Desai for taking the commendable step.

Mumbai
August 10, 2004

R.R. Singh
Former Director
Tata Institute of Social Sciences

Preface

As a direct outcome of undertaking the University Grants Commission-sponsored curriculum development project (1986 to 1990) and conducting refresher courses for teachers (since 1989) for social work education, the Tata Institute of Social Sciences (TISS) felt a need for a continued process for curriculum planning and teacher development for social work education. A Social Work Education and Practice Cell was, therefore, set up at the Institute in January 1992. The purpose of the Cell is training, research and resource development on methodology of social work education, through the following functions, at the local, national and international levels:

- Training of social work educators, at various levels and through various modes;
- Curriculum and resource development on social work education and its methodology for institutions, educators and students;
- Consultation, capacity building and collaboration with institutions for social work education, professional

associations and councils, and relevant government, voluntary and international organisations;

- Research on social work education and practice; and
- Development and dissemination of a data bank and a documentation centre on social work education, practice, professional associations and councils and literature on methodology of social work education.

The Cell has initiated to develop and disseminate a sourcebook series for education in social work and allied disciplines such as home science and development studies. These sourcebooks will be useful for the following groups:

- Academic institutions: to revise their curriculum in order to make it more relevant to meet the contemporary needs in the historical context and also local and national needs in the international context.
- Teachers: to plan and teach their subjects.
- Students: as learning handbooks.
- Practitioners: to update their knowledge, attitude and skills in the field.
- Academic staff colleges, teacher trainers and continuing education departments of these institutions: for conducting refresher training programmes for teachers, field supervisors and practitioners.
- Researchers: to identify the key concepts, theories and issues.

The series will be particularly useful for institutions where libraries are non-existent or have meagre resources. It will also benefit institutions in other countries that would like the international or cross-cultural orientation in their teaching, training and research pursuits.

Writing for this sourcebook on *Methodology of Progressive Social Work Education* has been a fascinating journey of reading, reflections and implementation and interactions with colleagues within and outside the TISS and students through different phases of my career as a social work educator.

- The chapter on 'Methodology of Progressive Social Work Knowledge Development' has its source in my work with a research unit in the Institute – the Unit for Family Studies – which was then linked to the Social Work Department of Family and Child Welfare. Besides carrying out social work research and publishing articles on it, I conducted workshops with students on how social work research has to apply social research methodology to improve social work practice. I also published a special issue of *The Indian Journal of Social Work* (*IJSW*) on 'Social Work Literature'.
- The chapter on 'Methodology of Progressive Social Work Knowledge Dissemination and Retrieval' emerged during my tenure as the Associate Editor of *IJSW*. My work in this position culminated in preparation of a Handbook of Management of *IJSW* and organising a National Workshop on Knowledge Development and Dissemination of Social Work Knowledge, on the 60th anniversary of the journal. A special issue of *IJSW* on this theme is in press.
- The chapters, relating to methodologies of building a perspective, curriculum development and teaching-learning and evaluation for progressive social work education, had their beginning in the form of handouts prepared for participants of Refresher Courses for Social Work Educators, conducted by the Cell. The chapter on 'Methodology of Building a Perspective for Progressive

Social Work Education' is adapted from a paper that I presented at the National Seminar on Standards for Assessment of Quality in Social Work Education.

- The chapter on 'Methodology of Progressive Training Programmes' has its source in conducting refresher courses as well as the training programme I organised with other colleagues on Life Enrichment Programme and preparation of sourcebooks for the same.

The draft sourcebook on Methodology of Social Work Education formed an important reference document for planning the National Seminar on Standards for Assessment of Quality in Social Work Education, organised by the TISS in November 2003, as well as the preparation of the Manual on Assessment and Accreditation of Social Work Education Programme, on invitation by the National Assessment and Accreditation Council. The sourcebook will further facilitate quality upgrading and maintenance of social work education.

The encouragement and support that I received from Prof. R.R. Singh, Director of the Institute, while preparing this sourcebook is gratefully acknowledged. I am also thankful to him for honouring the sourcebook by writing the Foreword for the same. Lastly, but most importantly, this endeavour would have not been possible without feedback from colleagues within and outside the Institute and students.

Murli Desai
Author of the Sourcebook
Chief Editor of the Sourcebook Series on Social Work Education
Professor and Head, Social Work Education and Practice Cell
Tata Institute of Social Sciences

Chapter 1

Introduction to Methodology of Progressive Social Work Education

INTRODUCTION

Successful teacher performance is generally assessed in the following areas:

- Teaching preparation and procedures;
- Classroom management;
- Knowledge of subject or academic preparation; and
- Personal characteristics and professional responsibility.

However, teachers go through four developmental stages to achieve success in these areas: survival, consolidation, renewal and maturity, as discussed below (Katz, 1972, cited from Stroot, Keil, Stedman, Lohr, Faust, Schincariol-Randall, Sullivan, Czerniak, Kuchcinski, Orel and Richter, 1998).

Survival

In the first stage of survival, the major concern of the teachers is coping on a daily basis, as teachers begin to question their personal and professional competence and their desire to teach. Teachers in this stage are also very self-centred and when they are able to teach, they focus on the act of teaching without considering whether or not the students are learning.

Consolidation

In the consolidation stage, teachers begin to focus on instruction and the needs of individual students. While observing a teacher in the consolidation stage, it is common to see the majority of students well-managed and the instructional activities meeting the needs of the average student in that class. Students who have special behavioural problems may still be disruptive, and though the individual needs of students are beginning to be recognised, the teacher is still struggling to find ways to meet special needs.

Renewal

In the third stage of renewal, teachers become competent in the practice of teaching children. Activities and patterns previously established become routine and boring, and teachers look for new ideas that provide variety in the teaching setting.

Maturity

The final stage of maturity occurs when teachers begin to ask questions of themselves and their teaching that focus on insights, perspectives and beliefs of teaching and children. Teachers in the maturity stage are still interested in new ideas and resources; however, they begin to ask deeper and more abstract questions about their philosophy of teaching and the impact they may be making in and out of the school setting.

Teachers need orientation courses in methodology of social work education to move from the survival to the consolidation stage. They need refresher courses in the renewal stage to enter the maturity stage. This chapter discusses the objectives of training social work educators, the foundation of life skills needed by social work educators, the methodology of social work education and the methodology of training social work educators.

OBJECTIVES OF TRAINING SOCIAL WORK EDUCATORS

Social work educators in India generally minimally have one of the degrees in social work, and often two or all, that is, Bachelor's, Master's and PhD degrees in this discipline. They may or may not have field experience, but would be expected to supervise participants in their fieldwork practicum. They may have just begun teaching or may have been teaching for some or more years. Initially, they also need knowledge, attitude and skills with reference to the methodology of social work education. They need to update their knowledge, attitude and skills of social work, after what they learnt as students, especially in the subjects that they teach, supervise participants and/or do research. As of now, teaching in higher education does not require a degree/certificate in teaching methodology. However, the University Grants Commission (UGC) requires lecturers in higher education to undergo orientation courses when they join and refresher courses after two years of working as a lecturer.

Following are the objectives as laid down by the UGC for teacher training in general:

1. Analyse the significance of higher education in the local, national and global context of society and development;
2. Understand the philosophy of education, education psychology and technology;
3. Develop technology of education; and
4. Promote development of personality, initiative and creativity.

Following may be the objectives specific to orientation training courses for social work educators:

Knowledge Objectives

- Critically understand the role played by the system of higher education in the local, national and global context of society and development; and
- Gain knowledge of theories of learning and group dynamics.

Attitude Objectives

- Treat participants and the community as partners in the process of learning and development; and
- Make a commitment to liberatory praxis, that is an ongoing process of moving between a critical perspective, one's teaching practices, evaluative reflection on the liberating or dominating aspects of teaching and back again to a critical perspective.

Skill Objectives

- Obtain skills in building a perspective for social work education, curriculum development, teaching and evaluation, fieldwork supervision, field action projects, conducting training programmes, social work research and publication, consultancy on social work, social welfare and development and contribution to social work professional associations;

- Develop skills of preparation of tools of teaching-learning and evaluation; and
- Promote an egalitarian, participatory and democratic management of the social work educational system.

In addition to the above objectives, refresher training courses for social work educators may also aim at obtaining an update on multidisciplinary knowledge, values and skills with reference to specific social work subjects or subject modules and fieldwork practicum.

FOUNDATION OF LIFE SKILLS FOR SOCIAL WORK EDUCATORS

Life skills training provides a foundation of integration of critical awareness, values and life skills, essential for the role of social work educators.

According to the document on 'Partners in Life Skills Education: Conclusions from a United Nations Inter-Agency Meeting' produced by the Mental Health Promotion and Policy Team in the World Health Organisation (WHO)'s Department of Mental Health (1999), "Life skills education is designed to facilitate the practice and reinforcement of psychological skills in a culturally and developmentally appropriate way; it contributes to the promotion of personal and social development, the prevention of health and social problems, and the protection of human rights." The organisations joining WHO in this effort were United Nations AIDS,

United Nations High Commission for Refugees, United Nations Children's Fund and United Nations Fund for Population Activities. The consensus among the participants was that "life skills" refers in particular to psycho-social skills, such as self-awareness, problem-solving, critical thinking and interpersonal skills. It does not necessarily include physical or motor skills or skills for livelihood/job.

Objectives of Life Skills Training

Life skills training may be defined as an experiential and participatory training programme that focuses on a process of reflecting and rethinking of one's assumptions, attitudes and skills, through the experiential methods, leading to development of value-based critical awareness and psycho-social skills. It aims at the integration of the following awareness, values and skills in one's life:

1. Develop critical awareness of the dynamics of physical, mental, emotional and social aspects of self, through the life span;
2. Imbibe the values of human dignity, harmony with nature, human rights, democratic participation, diversity and pluralism, equity and equality, justice and peace; and
3. Learn psycho-social skills for development of physical, mental, emotional and social aspects of self.

Modules of Life Skills Training

Life skills training is organised into the following modules:

1. Enrichment of Self-Awareness and Self-Esteem
2. Enrichment of Creative and Critical Thinking

3. Enrichment of Emotional Health
4. Coping with Negative Emotions
5. Enrichment of Interpersonal Communication
6. Enrichment of Social Interactions and Relationships

The units under each of these modules are listed below:

Module on Enrichment of Self-Awareness and Self-Esteem

The Module on Self-Awareness and Self-Esteem may include the following units:

- Introduction to Self-Awareness and Self-Esteem
- Self-Awareness
- Self-Identity and Self-Acceptance
- Self-Esteem
- Self-Confidence and Assertiveness

Module on Enrichment of Creative and Critical Thinking

The Module on Enrichment of Creative and Critical Thinking may be introduced after the Module on Self-Awareness and Self-Esteem and include the following units:

- Creative Thinking
- Critical Thinking
- Understanding Defense Mechanisms and Undertaking Self-Responsibility
- Time Management
- Decision-Making

Module on Enrichment of Emotional Health

The Module on Enrichment of Emotional Health needs to be introduced after the Module on Self-Awareness and Self-Esteem and may include the following units:

- Introduction to Emotions
- Awareness of Types of Emotions
- Positive Thinking
- Enhancing Happiness and Joy
- Capacity for Unconditional Love

Module on Coping with Negative Emotions

The Module on Coping with Negative Emotions should be introduced after the Module on Self-Awareness and Self-Esteem. It includes the following units:

- Problem-Solving
- Coping with Anger
- Coping with Fear, Anxiety and Stress
- Coping with Sadness, Hurt and Depression

Module on Enrichment of Interpersonal Communication

The Module on Enrichment of Interpersonal Communication may be introduced after the Modules on Self-Awareness and Self-Esteem and Enrichment of Emotional Health. It may include the following units:

- Introduction to Interpersonal Communication
- Enrichment of Use of Verbal Language
- Enrichment of Body Language
- Assertive and Open Communication
- Sensitive Listening
- Enrichment of Giving and Receiving Feedback

Module on Enrichment of Social Interactions and Relationships

The Module on Enrichment of Social Interactions and Relationships needs to be introduced after the Modules on Self-Awareness and Self-Esteem and Enrichment of Emotional Health. It may include the following units:

- Introduction to Enrichment of Social Interactions and Relationships
- Overcoming Shyness
- Recognition of Strengths
- Celebrating Differences with Others
- Sensitivity, Empathy and Support
- Win/Win Approach
- Conflict Management
- Enrichment of Teamwork
- Sensitivity to Marginalisation of Vulnerable Groups

Methodology of Life Skills Training

As stated earlier, life skills training is a participatory and experiential training that focuses on a process of reflecting and rethinking of one's assumptions, attitudes and skills, through the experiential methods, leading to development of critical awareness and psycho-social life skills.

METHODOLOGY OF SOCIAL WORK EDUCATION

The methodology of social work education may mainly include the following six components, which are covered in details in this sourcebook:

Methodology of Building a Perspective for Progressive Social Work Education

- Determination of the social work paradigm and the curricular ideologies for social work education;
- Analysis of the socio-economic-political realities;
- Identification of the values and goals of social work profession;
- Understanding the ethics and mission of social work education;
- Building the objectives of social work education; and
- Formulating a conceptual framework of subjects for social work education.

Methodology of Curriculum Development for Progressive Social Work Education

- Curriculum development by levels of courses;
- Curriculum development of class-work;
- Curriculum development of fieldwork practicum;
- Curriculum development of project report; and
- Development of a system of curriculum review.

Methodology of Teaching-Learning and Evaluation in Progressive Social Work Education

- Theories and stages of learning;
- Skills, methods and tools of teaching-learning; and
- Methods of evaluation.

Methodology of Progressive Training Programmes

- Training methods;

- Facilitation techniques; and
- Planning a training programme.

Methodology of Progressive Social Work Knowledge Development

- Concept and need for social work knowledge;
- Influence of progressive ideologies on social work knowledge;
- Methodology of social work research; and
- Ethics of social work research.

Methodology of Progressive Social Work Knowledge Dissemination and Retrieval

- Methodology of publication; and
- Methodology of retrieval of social work knowledge.

Besides, the following two components may also be included in the curriculum for training of social work educators, although these are not discussed in this sourcebook:

Methodology of Progressive Social Work Outreach Programmes

- Continuing and extension education;
- Consultancy on social work, welfare and development;
- Field action projects; and
- Contribution to social work professional associations.

Management of Social Work Education

- Management of infrastructure and learning resources for social work education;

- Management of student-related matters; and
- Organisational management of social work education.

METHODOLOGY OF TRAINING SOCIAL WORK EDUCATORS

For the methodology of training social work educators, refer to the experiential and participatory methodology of training, training methods, facilitation techniques and planning a training programme as discussed in the chapter on 'Methodology of Training Programmes'. Besides these, micro-teaching is an important method useful for training educators, which includes giving a short lecture, demonstration, or leading a discussion with your peers. The presentation is videotaped, and an evaluator gives you feedback on a number of different criteria. It is a time-proven method of teaching-learning and practising these skills. After participating, most participants feel that this is the very best way to learn to improve your teaching skills (www.fsu.edu/~ids/fac2002/ lecture.htm).

Chapter 2

Methodology of Building a Perspective for Progressive Social Work Education

INTRODUCTION

A curriculum is defined by Ornstein and Hunkins (1998) as a plan for action, a written document, which includes strategies for achieving desired goals or ends. Curriculum development is the process, the syntactical structure and the interpersonal dynamics of decision-making about curriculum planning. Curriculum design is the product, the substantive entity, and the end-result of the decision-making process (Gay, 1989). It is the organisational pattern or structure of a curriculum. It is determined by decisions made at two different levels of development: a broad level, which involves basic value choices, and a specific level, which involves the technical planning and implementation of curricular elements. At the broader level of decision-making, curriculum design is influenced by the choice of the data source or sources, which the developer chooses to emphasise (Klein, 1989). According to Lawton (1975, cited from Gay, 1989), curricula are made up of those particular aspects of life, knowledge, attitudes and values, selected from the total culture of a society, for transmission to future generations, within the structure of educational systems.

The Second Review Committee Report on Social Work Education by the University Grants Commission (UGC, 1980) recommended that for planning social work curriculum, the goals might be identified on the basis of analyses of the social realities. The goals then need to be related to the tasks and functions of social workers, after which the objectives of the social work education may be stated. The content may then be identified which will lead to the objectives.

Every five years or so, the perspective for social work education needs to be reviewed through workshops organised with all the faculty members of the institution for social work education, alumni, employers and other institutions for social work education, for a comprehensive review and renewal of the curriculum, including its ideological approach, aim, objectives and subject framework, and the goals for social work profession in the context of changing social realities. This chapter discusses the following steps for building and reviewing the perspective for social work education:

- Determination of the social work paradigm and the relevant curricular ideologies for social work education;
- Analysis of the contemporary socio-economic-political realities;
- Identification of the goals of social work profession;
- Understanding the ethics and mission of social work education;
- Building the objectives of social work education; and

- Formulating a conceptual framework of subjects for social work education.

SOCIAL WORK PARADIGMS

A paradigm is a system of beliefs about reality. It substantially defines what is an appropriate area in which to seek answers to the questions that we have about reality. Paradigm shift is the transition from one system of beliefs about reality to another (Courneyer and Klein, 2000). Social work paradigms range from the clinical to the ecological, to the progressive.

Clinical Social Work

In 1984, the NASW defined clinical social work as professional application of social work theory and methods to the treatment and prevention of psycho-social dysfunction, disability or impairment including emotional and mental disorders (Swensen, 1995). According to the clinical social work paradigm, some people cannot adjust to the larger forces due to psycho-social problems. Clients are considered deviants with a dysfunctional condition (Parsons, Jorgensen and Hernandez, 1994).

Ecological Social Work

In the ecological social work paradigm, problems are seen as deficits in the environment, as dysfunctional transactions between systems, rather than a disease located within the individual. Problems are not viewed as an attribute of people; these are viewed as an attribute of their social situation (Hartman and Laird, 1983). With its emphasis on the environmental context, it has also sparked off efforts to understand culturally specific populations and to create culture-appropriate frameworks for practice (Pinderhughes, 1995). The problem's embeddedness from micro to macro systems and linkages between these systems are understood. Oppression and discrimination issues are identified based on ethnicity, gender, class, age and sexual orientation (Parsons and others, 1994).

Progressive Social Work

Progressive social workers may identify themselves as radicals, socialists, leftists, political practitioners or activists. They are critical of the injustices in institutions, systems, beliefs and social practices that cause the poorest and most vulnerable groups to suffer. They articulate these social injustices into "public issues" instead of adopting a strictly case-by-case perspective that views the outcomes of social injustices as "personal troubles" those that individuals must cope with or adapt to (Mills, 1959, cited from Bombyk, 1995). Progressive social workers strive to alter oppressive institutions, systems, beliefs and practices fundamentally by initiating social changes targeted at these public issues. They also work directly with individuals to help them heal from their wounds, to educate them about their life choices and strategies, and to assist then as they determine their futures (Bombyk, 1995).

Radical social work is based on the ideology that the most effective way to achieve goals of equality and solutions to social problems is to eliminate or make major changes in the existing institutions. It includes techniques for peaceably bringing about these changes, including passive resistance, demonstrations, strikes and political and social activism (Barker, 1987).

CURRICULUM IDEOLOGIES

Social work education needs to draw from the curriculum ideologies relevant to the social work paradigm being followed. Curriculum ideologies are value premises about what should be taught, for what and why, from which decisions about practical educational matters are made (Toohey, 1999). Some of these ideologies include the traditional or discipline-based, personal relevance or experiential, socially critical and the critical pedagogical approaches, as discussed below:

Ideology of the Traditional or Discipline-based Approach

The design of most university and college courses traditionally follows the structure of knowledge in the discipline. Programmes of study are divided into units and topics based on important concepts, and each topic is structured in some rational manner. The important point to notice here is, that whatever logical base is used to structure the course – chronological, causal, scale of operations, form of expression – it exists within the subject matter itself and the way in which the discipline is usually structured. It is not related to student interests, the way people learn or the ways in which problems present them in everyday life (Toohey, 1999).

In this perspective on the curriculum, knowledge is conceived as existing independently. It forms a body of theory, which has been developed, refined and tested over time. It exists in books and published records, waiting to be accessed by students. Most emphasis is placed on the technical, rational and managerial aspects of knowledge, which help to give greater control over the world, rather than on personal or expressive knowledge. There is a strong leaning towards abstract and theoretical knowledge, to the point where even highly relevant skills such as report writing or library research may not be considered appropriate to be taught within the course (Toohey, 1999).

Paulo Freire (1972) criticised the traditional approach as the 'banking' approach, where the teacher knows everything and the student knows nothing, so the teacher teaches and the students are taught, as though the teacher is the depositor and the students the depositories. According to him, knowledge emerges only through invention and reinvention, through the restless, impatient continuing hopeful inquiry human beings pursue in the world, with the world and with each other.

Ideology of the Experiential or Personal Relevance Approach

One of the most influential proponents of the experiential or personal relevance approach has been Malcolm Knowles, who put forward the idea that adult learners needed a different kind of educational approach from children. A fundamental tenet of his andragogical model is that adults do not learn for the sake of learning; they learn in order to be able to perform a task, solve a problem, or live in a more satisfying way. The chief implication of this assumption is the importance of organising learning experiences (the curriculum) around life situations rather than according to subject matter units (Toohey, 1999).

A climate conducive to learning is important in this approach, which would be characterised by mutual respect between teacher and students, encouragement of collaboration and support among students, and openness and authenticity on the part of the teacher. Students are likely to be involved in the planning of the curriculum so that it reflects their learning needs and they feel the commitment that comes with participation in decision-making. The role of the teacher in this process is to assist students to design and carry out their learning plans. The teacher may provide some information sessions (lectures), facilitate group work, arrange contacts with resource people and offer individual consultation for support and guidance (Toohey, 1999). Fieldwork practicum and continuing education for social work educators and practitioners need to draw from this approach to a large extent.

Ideology of the Socially Critical Approach

The socially critical approach is the most relevant approach for progressive social work education, as it aims to develop a critical consciousness in students so that they become aware of the present ills of society and are motivated to alleviate them. The socially critical approach to curriculum draws upon the work of critical theorists who believe that the institutions of society, including educational institutions, are created and moulded by social elites. The role of the critical theorists and the socially critical curriculum is to examine society, its institutions and its cultural products, and to expose the covert values that guide the way these work. Students and teacher engage together in understanding and critiquing social institutions or work on collaborative projects, which have some social significance (Toohey, 1999).

From a socially critical perspective, knowledge is constructed within our historical and cultural frameworks. Knowledge, according to the critical theorists, is historically, socially, economically and politically conditioned. The teacher's role is to help students understand where their own views have come from, to challenge pre-conceptions and to encourage them to consider other possibilities. Within a socially critical curriculum, a key question that students learn to ask is, "Whose interests are being served here?" As with the experiential or personal relevance orientation, the overall goal is to produce a graduate capable of self-realisation. The difference is that self-realisation is seen in a social context rather than as a purely individual matter. Collaborative work and group projects are likely to be encouraged, as are self and peer assessment (Toohey, 1999).

Ideology of Critical Pedagogy

Similar to the socially critical approach, the critical pedagogical approach, influenced by Paulo Freire, is also very relevant to progressive social work. According to Boyce (1996), three assumptions serve as organising principles for critical pedagogy:

1. Education is not neutral, it either domesticates or liberates.
2. Society can be transformed by the engagement of critically conscious persons, through a process of deconstruction, reconstruction and transformation.
3. Praxis, which is an ongoing process of moving between text or theory, application, evaluative reflection, and back to theory, connects liberatory education with social transformation. Applied to teaching a subject critically, praxis involves moving between a critical perspective, one's teaching practices, evaluative reflection on the liberating and/or dominating aspects of the teaching, and back again to a critical and liberatory perspective. A commitment to praxis necessitates the reflective practice of teaching behaviours that demonstrate a critical

approach and increase one's effectiveness at creating a liberating learning environment.

Heany (1995) states that liberatory education is mutually supported learning for empowerment. It encourages learners to challenge and change the world, not merely uncritically adapt to it. The content and purpose of liberatory education is the collective responsibility of learners, teachers and the community alike who, through dialogue, seek political as well as economic empowerment. Whatever its formal structure or precise purpose, such education is a component of and subordinate to a liberatory praxis which seeks to transform the social order. Transforming actions in aggregate comprise a revolutionary stance, which simultaneously announces an egalitarian, participatory and democratic social order and denounces hierarchical, authoritarian and alienating systems of organisations. The content of liberatory education is both critical consciousness and the development of appropriate skills and competencies related to liberatory praxis. The governance of liberatory education reflects and anticipates the social order announced by its vision.

Post-modern concepts have enabled social work profession to examine the complexities of power in 'client'-worker relationship, reinforcement of mainstream middle class norms in assessment processes, and so on. These have helped social workers to create empowering relationships by deconstructing professional power, which stems from their position as bearers of particular ideologies and implementers of a social mandate, determined in the political arena (Dominelli, 2002). Similarly, social work educators have more power than social work students with reference to their age, knowledge and position. Attempts need to be made to equalise this power equation by treating students as partners in the learning process.

SOCIAL REALITIES

The knowledge emerging from development studies and exchange with action groups and social movements and non-government organisations indicates the following analysis of the contemporary social realities in the historical context and national realities in the international context. Historically, systemic discrimination of vulnerable groups, because of their sex, ethnicity, age, health, economic background, sexual orientation and such other attributes, resulted in marginalisation of women, dalits, tribals or indigenous people, children, youth, older persons, the labour class, persons with disabilities, mental or terminal illness, or varying sexual orientations, and others. The socio-economic-political institutions or systems of family, community and state, which are supposed to protect and enhance the security of the human person, have taken up a life of their own. Together with the corporate sector and the mass media, these institutions have reinforced such domination and marginalisation, violating people's basic rights to food and nutrition, water and sanitation, livelihood and employment, health, housing, environmental sustainability, and literacy and basic education.

The historical problems are aggravated by the production and consumption-based 'development' that created new hierarchies of the urban-organised versus the rural-unorganised, widening the disparities, within and between nations. Now, liberalisation, privatisation and globalisation, under the pressure of the international institutions, promote minimum government interference and consider market as the sole social regulator. The result of these processes has been found to be increased consumption, resulting in environmental devastation and the wiping out of cultural and biological diversity, much of it irretrievably lost, without compensation to those reliant on it. Mass media and corporate consumerist culture have been the main agents of commodification and homogenisation of cultural diversity. Domination of western science and methodology has swept away the indigenous knowledge systems and technologies based on centuries of experience. In such a scenario, poverty, social conflict, violence and environmental disasters are on the increase.

The emerging ideological approaches to counter these politico-economic forces are the second-wave feminism, multiculturalism, sustainability, promoting the values of social equity, local self-governance, democratic pluralism, people's participation and peaceful collaborative social dynamics. With the resurgence of the civil society in the form of action groups resulting in social movements, social work profession has a very significant role to play in partnership with the people-centred ideologies and groups.

VALUES AND GOALS OF SOCIAL WORK PROFESSION

Adapting from the Declaration of Ethics for Professional Social Workers (Bombay Association of Trained Social Workers, 2002), the values for life enrichment may comprise the following:

Values in Perception of People

Human worth and dignity: People have inherent worth and dignity, irrespective of their attributes and achievements, having the capability of change and development.

Harmony with Nature: People are part of the scheme of nature, needing to live in harmony with other forms of life.

Values as Goals for People

Human rights: Basic human needs such as food and water, health, livelihood, shelter, education, environmental security, family and community identity and interdependence are human rights.

Democratic pluralism: Democratisation of the socio-economic systems such as family, community, state, market and media, and also diversity and pluralism in ethnicity, culture, thought and choices.

Equity and equality: Equity and equality, non-hierarchy, non-discrimination and democratic pluralism of human groups in terms of attributes such as sex, race, nationality, colour, caste, religion, tribe, language, regional origin, gender, sexual orientation and other such factors, and condemnation of marginalisation and segregation among them.

Justice: Social, economic, political and legal justice, ensuring universal and equitable access to essential resources and protective safeguards for the marginalised people.

Values for Work with People

Professionalism: Attributes such as humility, honesty, integrity, trustworthiness, optimism and commitment to one's work; and people's participation, self-determination, cooperation and collaboration as the principles of interaction.

Solidarity with the marginalised people: Sensitivity and partnership with the marginalised people and recognising strengths in them.

Peace: Peace and non-violence for resolving conflicts with self, others and the environment. Peace is more than absence of violence. It encompasses non-violence, acceptance, fairness and communication.

In the backdrop of the contemporary social realities and the values of social work profession, the following may be elaborated as goals of progressive social work profession:

1. Promote values of human worth and dignity, harmony with nature, human rights, democratic pluralism, participation, equity and equality and justice.
2. Prevent and ameliorate the systemic discrimination and marginalisation of vulnerable groups because of their sex, ethnicity, age, health, economic background, sexual orientation and such other attributes, and recognise strengths in and facilitate inclusion of marginalised groups such as women, dalits, tribals/indigenous people, nomadic communities, landless and small farmers, pastoralists, the labour class, children, youth, older persons, and persons with disabilities, mental or terminal illness, or varying sexual orientations.
3. Work for promotion of basic human rights such as food and nutrition, water and sanitation, livelihood and employment, health, housing, environmental sustainability, literacy and basic education, and relief and rehabilitation of victims of displacement, social conflict and environmental disasters.
4. Identify linkages across and work for democratisation of the socio-economic-political systems of family, community, state, corporate sector and mass media, to prevent and ameliorate social problems, supported by participatory training, legal aid, advocacy and public interest litigations, conflict resolution in social

conflict situations, relief and rehabilitation in emergency situations, policy and programme planning and administration of non-profit organisations, monitoring and evaluation.

ETHICS AND MISSION OF SOCIAL WORK EDUCATION

Ethics of Social Work Education

According to the Declaration of Ethics for Professional Social Workers, prepared by the Social Work Educators' Forum of the Tata Institute of Social Sciences (1997) and revised by the Bombay Association of Trained Social Workers (2002), following are the best ethical responsibilities of professional social workers as educators and researchers:

- Are conversant with the learners' needs, readiness and goals, when teaching and training.
- Regularly update knowledge about social work profession in general and the subjects they teach, through field experience, update reading and training.
- Impart knowledge, inculcate attitudes and develop skills within the value framework of the profession, while teaching and training.
- Recognise the importance of partnership between practitioners and educators for the purpose of social work education and training.
- Develop a nurturing relationship with students, encouraging openness, critical inquiry and self-study.
- Undertake people-centred field action projects as a demonstration of innovative initiatives to promote the

well-being of people and for research and documentation, training and replication, whenever possible.

- Contribute to the knowledge base of social work education through practice wisdom, documentation as well as research.
- Expose the students to the professional associations and orient them about their role in developing and strengthening them.
- Carefully select the topic for research considering its possible consequences for those studied, when conducting a research.
- Do not cause the respondents any physical or mental discomfort, distress or harm, through research.
- Consider the informants of research as co-partners in understanding the phenomenon.
- Share their research objectives with them and get their informed and voluntary consent, respect their knowledge and attitude about their life situation, and share/interpret the findings with them.
- Protect the confidentiality of the information shared by them and use the findings for their benefit, by recommending and promoting policies and programmes concerning them.
- Provide information and referral services to them, as and when necessary, during the process of data collection.
- Dissociate from or do not engage in any research activity, which requires manipulation, distortion or falsification of data or findings.
- Acknowledge in their written work, the published as well as unpublished material, and discussions that have directly contributed to it.

Mission of Social Work Education

Drawing from the goals and ethics of progressive social work profession, the following mission may be identified for progressive social work education:

- Prepare qualified social work personnel and provide continuing education to them for social work practice, administration, education, training and research, within the value framework of the profession. The aim of social work education is imparting integration of social work knowledge, attitude and skills, relevant to the contemporary social realities, in the historical context, and local social realities, in the national and international context.
- Develop a critical consciousness in students, through a process of critical pedagogy, so that they become aware of the social ills of society and are motivated to alleviate them. The approach to be used is student-centred dialogical classroom teaching-learning, self-study, supervised fieldwork practicum and practice-based research.
- Undertake field action projects for demonstration of role of social work professionals and innovative social work practice, administration, training and practice-based research and provide fieldwork placement to students.
- Develop and disseminate knowledge for evidence-based social work practice, administration, education, training and research. The methodology to be used is an integration of knowledge and action, based on a critical inquiry into multidisciplinary and applied social science knowledge, practice wisdom, practice-based and participatory research, documentation of best practices, policy analysis and so on.

- Provide consultation on social work, welfare and development policies and programmes, teaching and research, to the voluntary, government, international and other academic organisations, and also strengthen professional associations in social work.
- Promote an egalitarian, participatory and democratic educational system and denounce a hierarchical, authoritarian and alienating educational system. Make a commitment to liberatory praxis, that is an ongoing process of moving between a critical perspective, one's teaching, field action, research, administration and consultation, and evaluative reflection and back again to a critical perspective.

OBJECTIVES OF SOCIAL WORK EDUCATION

Drawing from the mission of progressive social work education, the objectives of progressive social work education may be an integration of the following knowledge, attitude and skill areas:

Knowledge Objectives

The knowledge objectives of social work education may be to critically evaluate multidisciplinary knowledge and disaggregated data, to understand the contemporary reality in the historical context and local reality in the national and international context, with specific reference to the following aspects:

- Roles played by ideologies in the development of knowledge and alternate viewpoints by different stakeholders, including social workers;

- Dynamics of human development and behaviour in the context of the social systems such as family and community;
- Political economy of the corporate sector, mass media, state, political, legal and judicial systems and welfare and development policies and schemes, from local to national levels, influenced by international institutions;
- The process of systemic marginalisation of vulnerable groups and emerging social conflicts; and
- History, values and ethics, functions and methods of social work profession.

Attitude Objectives

The attitude objectives of social work education may be to develop critical self-awareness and reflection, with reference to the following attributes, values, sensitivities and ethical requirements of social work profession:

- Professional attributes such as humility, honesty, integrity, trustworthiness, optimism and commitment to one's work;
- Values of human worth and dignity, harmony with nature, human rights, democratic pluralism, participation, equity and equality, justice, people's participation, self-determination, cooperation and collaboration;
- Sensitivity, solidarity and partnership with marginalised groups such as women, dalits, tribals/indigenous people, nomadic communities, landless and small farmers, pastoralists, the labour class, children, youth, older persons, persons with disabilities, mental or terminal illness, or varying sexual orientations and others, and recognising strengths in them;

- Peace and non-violence for resolving conflicts with self, others and the environment; and
- Ethical behaviour with reference to self, marginalised groups, society and the state, colleagues and the employing organisation, education, training and research, and towards the profession.

Skill Objectives

The skill objectives of social work education may be to develop skills of working with people, processes and systems, in the following areas:

- Self-awareness, self-esteem, creative, critical and positive thinking, emotional health, interpersonal communication and social interactions and relationships;
- Basic methods of work with individuals and the socio-economic-political systems of family, community, state, corporate sector, mass media and non-profit organisations, democratise them, drawing linkages across them, to prevent and ameliorate individual and social problems; and
- Support methods of monitoring and evaluation, practice-based and participatory research, participatory training, conflict resolution and disaster management.

CONCEPTUAL FRAMEWORK OF SUBJECTS IN SOCIAL WORK EDUCATION

Drawing from the objectives of progressive social work education, a conceptual framework of subjects may be developed. From this framework, a social work programme may select subjects according to their specific mission, objectives and curriculum structure. The following are proposed as the subject modules in social work curriculum planning:

Modules of Foundation Social Science Subjects

Social work students need to have a foundation of social sciences, at the graduation level and/or interdisciplinary and applied social sciences, at the post-graduation level. Social work students may be required to take these subjects from the respective departments of their university, or through visiting faculty, or the social work faculty may teach these subjects.

Modules of Basic Subjects

The basic subjects for social work education consist of the core social work subjects, subjects on governance, welfare and development and the social work fieldwork practicum.

Modules of Optional Subjects

The modules of optional subjects for social work education comprise of subjects from humanities and other allied sciences and issues and intervention for sector-wise human rights, human rights of marginalised groups and human rights in social conflict and emergency situations.

Modules of Social Work Specialisations/Concentrations

No specialisations/concentrations should be offered at the BSW level. If specialisations/concentrations are offered at the MSW level, the first year should mainly provide the foundation, basic and optional subjects. Students should be provided adequate information and guidance to make an informed and planned selection of the specialisation/concentrations to be offered in the second year.

As of now, the common social work specialisations offered are by a social system and a marginalised group (Family and Child Welfare), sectors (Medical and Psychiatric Social Work and Criminology, Correctional Administration, Personnel Management and Industrial Relations and Urban and Rural Community Development) and a function (Social Welfare Administration). This classification of specialisations has led to overlaps and needs to be re-rationalised. Following are classification alternatives suggested for specialisations or concentrations. Whatever the specialisation structure selected, a generalist stream should also be offered.

Conceptual Framework of Social Work Subjects

1. Foundation of Social Science Subjects	
1.1 Social Sciences • Psychology • Sociology • Anthropology • Political Science • Economics	**1.2 Interdisciplinary and Applied Social Sciences** • Human Development • Applied Psychology • Society and Social Systems • Tribal Anthropology • Political Economy • Demography and Population Dynamics • Women's Studies • Dalit Studies • Development Studies
↓	

2. Basic Subjects		
2.2. Governance, Welfare and Development	**2.1. Core Social Work Subjects**	**2.3. Social Work Fieldwork Practicum**
• Welfare Policies and Schemes • Development Policies and Schemes • The United Nations System and Globalisation • Development Alternatives • Local Self-Governance • Social Legislation, Legal Systems and Legal Advocacy	*2.1.1 Ideologies, Values and Social Work* • History of Ideologies, Social Change and Social Work • Social Justice, Human Rights and Social Work *2.1.2 Approaches of Social Work* • Generalist Social Work • Clinical Social Work • Social Action *2.1.3 Methods of Social Work with Social Systems* • Family Social Work • Community Social Work • Corporate Social Responsibility and Social Work • Mass Media, Communication and Social Work • Administration of Non-Profit Organisations *2.1.4 Support Methods of Social Work* • Social Work Research • Participatory Training and Field Instruction • Conflict Resolution and Disaster Management	

<table>
<tr><td colspan="2">3. Optional Subjects</td></tr>
<tr><td>3.1 Humanities

• English Language and Literature
• Hindi/ Local Language and Literature
• Philosophy/ Fine Arts/ History</td><td>3.2 Other Allied Sciences

• Food and Nutrition
• Health and Hygiene
• Environment Studies</td></tr>
<tr><td>3.3 Issues and Intervention for Sectorwise Human Rights

• Physical Health
• Mental Health
• Reproductive and Sexual Health
• Literacy and Basic Education
• Food and Water Security
• Livelihood and Employment
• Credit and Income Generation
• Environmental Sustainability
• Land and Housing
• Sustainable Agriculture, Forestry and Animal Husbandry
• Consumer Protection</td><td>3.4 Issues and Intervention for Human Rights of Marginalised Groups

• Children, Adolescents and Youth
• Older Persons
• Persons with Disabilities
• Women
• Dalits
• Labour
• Tribals, Nomadic Communities and Pastoralists</td></tr>
<tr><td>3.5 Issues and Intervention for Human Rights in Social Conflict and Emergency Situations

• Family Violence
• Substance Abuse
• Trafficking and Sale of Persons
• Communalism and Collective Violence
• Conflict with Law
• Displacement and Refugees
• Environmental Disasters</td><td></td></tr>
<tr><td colspan="2">↓</td></tr>
</table>

4. Social Work Specialisations/Concentrations	
4.1 Classification by Approaches to Social Work Intervention • Clinical Social Work Approach • Social Action Approach • Generalist (clinical and social action) Social Work Approach	**4.2 Classification by Levels of Social Work Practice** • Micro (direct) Social Work Practice • Macro (policy and programme planning) Social Work Practice • Generalist (micro-macro) Social Work Practice
4.3 Classification by Issues and Social Work Intervention for Sectorwise Human Rights • Social Work for Health • Social Work for Environmental Sustainability • Social Work in Social Conflict and Emergency Situations • Social Work for Rural Development • Social Work for Urban Development • Generalist Social Work (cutting across sectors)	**4.4 Classification by Issues and Social Work Intervention for Human Rights of Marginalised Groups** • Gender Aware Social Work • Social Work with Urban Marginalised • Social Work with Rural Marginalised • Social Work with Children, Adolescents and Youth • Gerontological Social Work • Social Work with Persons with Disabilities • Generalist Social Work (cutting across all the groups)

Note

This Chapter on Methodology of Building a Perspective for Progressive Social Work Education, is adapted from a paper that I presented at the National Seminar on Standards for Assessment of Quality in Social Work Education, organised by the Tata Institute of Social Sciences in November 2003, on invitation by the National Assessment and Accreditation Council.

Chapter 3

Methodology of Curriculum Development for Progressive Social Work Education

INTRODUCTION

A good curriculum design should have consistency and logical organisation. When the curriculum possesses high internal consistency, it will have a greater potential for having the desired impact upon the students. If the data sources and curricular elements are not treated in a consistent manner and have no clearly defined relationships to each other, the design of the curriculum will be confused and the potential impact upon students will be lessened (Klein, 1989).

According to Ornstein and Hunkins (1998), a curriculum should foster cumulative and continuous learning, or what is known as the vertical relationship among curricular areas. It should be based on the logic of the subject matter and on the way in which individuals process knowledge. The principles of sequencing according to them are:

1. Simple to complex learning;

2. Prerequisite learning, meaning some learning must be grasped before other learning can be comprehended;
3. Whole to part learning, meaning the content is presented first in an overview fashion to furnish students with a general idea of the situation before the specifics; and
4. Chronological learning.

The criteria for selecting the curricular content, according to Ornstein and Hunkins (1998), are self-sufficiency, significance to the overall goals, validity or authenticity, interest or meaningfulness to the learner, utility, learnability and feasibility, in the light of the resources available.

Based on the progressive social work paradigm, curricular ideologies, ethics, mission, objectives and subject framework of social work education, the following aspects of curriculum development for progressive social work education are discussed in this chapter:

- Overall curriculum development by levels of courses;
- Curriculum development of class-work;
- Curriculum development of fieldwork practicum;
- Curriculum development of project report;
- Curriculum development of co-curricular activities; and
- Development of a system of curriculum review.

OVERALL CURRICULUM DEVELOPMENT BY LEVELS OF COURSES

Levels, Curriculum Structure and Modalities of Social Work Education

Levels of social work education: Social work education is provided at the para-professional, Bachelor's (BSW), Master's

(MSW) and MPhil and PhD levels, requiring increasing order of advancement of curriculum development. Curriculum by levels of academic courses needs to be developed in a sequential manner, with reference to the minimum educational qualifications, aim, objectives and structure. Subjects may be selected from the subject framework, according to the level.

Curriculum structure: The curriculum structure for social work education includes the components of linkages across class-work, fieldwork practicum and project report; allocation of credits, hours and marks; and their scheduling into semesters and years. According to the UGC regulations (2003) regarding the minimum standards of instruction through formal education, the number of actual teaching days should not be less than 180 in an academic year, implying 90 days or 15 weeks per term or semester. These regulations also require that the contact teaching shall not be less than 30 hours per week and time provided for practicals, fieldwork, library, utilisation of computer and other such facilities shall not be less than 10 hours per week. This amounts to a total of 40 hours a week, or seven hours per day (9 to 4 or 10 to 5) for six days a week or eight hours per day (9 to 5) for five days a week.

According to the Second Review Committee Report of UGC (1980), every MSW course requires a minimum of 15 hours of fieldwork practicum. This implies that the remaining 25 hours should cover class-work, project report and co-curricular activities.

Modality: Social work education may be offered as full-time programmes or as part-time/evening modular programmes. The mode of the academic programme may be campus-based, distance education or mixed.

Para-professional Programme

Minimum educational qualifications: Candidates who have a minimum of Higher Secondary or Junior College qualification can be eligible for admission to the para-professional certificate programme in social work.

Aim and objectives: The aim of the para-professional certificate programme may be training for field level social work tasks. The objectives may be as follows:

Knowledge Objectives

The knowledge objectives may be to critically analyse multidisciplinary knowledge, with reference to the following aspects:

- Dynamics of human development and behaviour;
- Roles played by the social systems of family and community; and
- Systemic marginalisation of vulnerable groups.

Attitude Objectives

The attitude objectives may be to develop critical self-awareness, with reference to the following ideological and ethical requirements of social work profession:

- Professional attributes such as humility, honesty, integrity, trustworthiness, optimism and commitment to one's work;
- Values of human worth and dignity, harmony with nature, human rights, democratic pluralism, participation, equity and equality, justice, people's participation, self-determination, cooperation and collaboration;

- Sensitivity, solidarity and partnership with marginalised groups such as women, dalits, tribals/indigenous people, the labour class, children, youth, older persons, persons with disabilities or mental or terminal illness and others, and recognising strengths in them;
- Peace and non-violence for resolving conflicts with self, others and the environment; and
- Ethical behaviour with reference to self, marginalised groups, colleagues and the employing organisation.

Skill Objectives

The skill objectives may be to develop skills of working with people, processes and systems, in the following areas:

- Self-awareness, self-esteem, creative, critical and positive thinking, emotional health, interpersonal communication and social interactions and relationships; and
- Basic methods of work with individuals and the socio-economic-political systems of family, community and non-profit organisations, democratise them, drawing linkages across them, to prevent and ameliorate individual and social problems.

BSW Programme

Minimum educational qualifications: Candidates who have a minimum of Higher Secondary or Junior College qualification can be eligible for admission to the BSW programme.

Total period and annual certification: The BSW programme needs to be planned for three years of full-time study, providing for annual certification as follows:

	Type of Certification in Social Work
Completion of 1st year	Para-professional Certificate in Social Work
Completion of 2nd year	Para-professional Diploma in Social Work
Completion of 3rd year	Bachelor's Degree in Social Work

Aim and objectives: The aim of the BSW programme may be to prepare generalist social work practitioners, who can work with individuals, families, groups and communities, for promotion of their rights to food and nutrition, health and literacy and basic education. The objectives of the BSW programme may be as follows:

Knowledge Objectives

The knowledge objectives may be to critically analyse multidisciplinary knowledge, to understand the contemporary reality in the historical context with reference to the following aspects:

- Dynamics of human development and behaviour;
- Roles played by the social systems of family and community;
- Political economy of the corporate sector, mass media, state, political, legal and judicial systems and welfare and development policies and schemes, from local to national levels, influenced by international institutions;
- Systemic marginalisation of vulnerable groups and emerging social conflicts; and
- History, values and ethics, functions and methods of social work profession.

Attitude Objectives

The attitude objectives may be to develop critical self-awareness, with reference to the following ideological and ethical requirements of social work profession:

- Professional attributes such as humility, honesty, integrity, trustworthiness, optimism and commitment to one's work;
- Values of human worth and dignity, harmony with nature, human rights, democratic pluralism, participation, equity and equality, justice, people's participation, self-determination, cooperation and collaboration;
- Sensitivity, solidarity and partnership with marginalised groups such as women, dalits, tribals/indigenous people, nomadic communities, landless and small farmers, pastoralists, the labour class, children, youth, older persons, persons with disabilities, mental or terminal illness, or varying sexual orientations, and others and recognising strengths in them;
- Peace and non-violence for resolving conflicts with self, others and the environment; and
- Ethical behaviour with reference to self, marginalised groups, society and the state, colleagues and the employing organisation, education, training and research, and towards the profession.

Skill Objectives

The skill objectives may be to develop skills of working with people, processes and systems, in the following areas:

- Self-awareness, self-esteem, creative, critical and positive thinking, emotional health, interpersonal communication and social interactions and relationships;
- Basic methods of work with individuals and the socio-economic-political systems of family, community, state, corporate sector, mass media and non-profit organisations, democratise them, drawing linkages across them, to prevent and ameliorate individual and social problems; and
- Support methods of monitoring and evaluation, practice-based and participatory research, participatory training, conflict resolution and disaster management.

MSW Programme

Minimum educational qualifications: Eligibility for admission to the MSW programme requires a Bachelor's degree, preferably in social sciences, home science, or social work. In order to prevent unproductive repetition in the MSW programme, for those with a Bachelor's degree in social work, the Master's programme must develop explicit policies and procedures such as course waivers, substitutions, exemptions, or advanced placement.

Total period and annual certification: The MSW programme needs to be planned for two years of full-time study. Those who want to exit after a year, may be given a post-graduate certificate in social work.

Aim and objectives: The aim of the MSW programme may be to prepare advanced generalist social work practitioners, with a focussed training in a field of specialisation or in one or two areas of concentrations. Advanced competencies include differentiated, discriminating and self-critical practice, with a high degree of autonomy and skill, and ability to refine and advance the qualities of their practice, as well as that of the social work profession.

The following are the objectives of the MSW programme, assuming that the students come without a BSW degree:

Knowledge Objectives

The knowledge objectives may be to critically analyse multidisciplinary knowledge, with reference to the following aspects:

- Roles played by ideologies in the development of knowledge and alternate viewpoints by different stake-holders, including social workers;
- Dynamics of human development and behaviour in the context of the social systems, such as family and community;
- Political economy of the corporate sector, mass media, state, political, legal and judicial systems and welfare and development policies and schemes, from local to national levels, influenced by international institutions;
- The process of systemic marginalisation of vulnerable groups and emerging social conflicts; and
- History, values and ethics, functions and methods of social work profession.

Attitude Objectives

The attitude objectives may be to develop critical self-awareness, with reference to the following ideological and ethical requirements of social work profession:

- Professional attributes such as humility, honesty, integrity, trustworthiness, optimism and commitment to one's work;
- Values of human worth and dignity, harmony with nature, human rights, democratic pluralism, participation, equity and equality, justice, people's participation, self-determination, cooperation and collaboration;
- Sensitivity, solidarity and partnership with marginalised groups such as women, dalits, tribals/indigenous people, nomadic communities, landless and small farmers, pastoralists, the labour class, children, youth, older persons, persons with disabilities, mental or terminal illness, or varying sexual orientations and others, and recognising strengths in them;
- Peace and non-violence for resolving conflicts with self, others and the environment; and
- Ethical behaviour with reference to self, marginalised groups, society and the state, colleagues and the employing organisation, education, training and research, and towards the profession.

Skill Objectives

The skill objectives may be to develop the following people-centred skills:

- Self-awareness, self-esteem, creative, critical and positive thinking, emotional health, interpersonal communication and social interactions and relationships;
- Basic methods of work with individuals and the socio-economic-political systems of family, community, state, corporate sector, mass media and non-profit organisations, democratise them, drawing linkages across

them, to prevent and ameliorate individual and social problems; and

- Support methods of monitoring and evaluation, practice-based and participatory research, participatory training, conflict resolution and disaster management.

Integrated Programme

A five-year integrated programme for social work education may be planned, providing scope for a multi-entry and multi-exit system, where students can enter, move out of the system with a certification and come in again with experience at any point of time. The annual certification may be provided as follows:

	Type of Certification in Social Work
Completion of 1st year	Para-professional Certificate in Social Work
Completion of 2nd year	Para-professional Diploma in Social Work
Completion of 3rd year	Bachelor's Degree in Social Work
Completion of 4th year	Post-graduate Certificate in Social Work
Completion of 5th year	Master's Degree in Social Work

Post-MA Certificate/Diploma Programmes

Social work programmes, which offer an MSW course, may also offer a one-year post-MA certificate/diploma course for specialisation in a social work function such as social welfare/development policy planning and administration, social work research, social work education, or for advanced social work practice in a specialised field, or for international social work.

MPhil and PhD Programmes

Minimum educational qualifications: Candidates with a minimum of a MSW degree and a minimum of two years of experience as social work practitioners may be eligible for admission to the Master of Philosophy and Doctor of Philosophy (MPhil and PhD) programmes in social work.

Aim and objectives: The aim of the MPhil and PhD programmes in social work may be to prepare social work educators and researchers. The objectives may be as follows:

Knowledge Objectives

The knowledge objectives may be to critically evaluate multidisciplinary knowledge and disaggregated data, with reference to the following aspects:

- Analysis of the epistemology of research methodologies and practice theories; and
- Review of theories on a select marginalised group and their select issue, their application in the Indian situation and the relevant research methods.

Attitude Objectives

The attitude objectives may be to develop critical self-awareness and reflection, with reference to the following ideological and ethical requirements of social work profession:

- Professional attributes such as humility, honesty, integrity, trustworthiness, optimism and commitment to one's work;
- Values of human worth and dignity, harmony with nature, human rights, democratic pluralism,

participation, equity and equality, justice, people's participation, self-determination, cooperation and collaboration;

- Sensitivity, solidarity and partnership with marginalised groups such as women, dalits, tribals/indigenous people, nomadic communities, landless and small farmers, pastoralists, the labour class, children, youth, older persons, persons with disabilities, mental or terminal illness, or varying sexual orientations and others, and recognising strengths in them;
- Peace and non-violence for resolving conflicts with self, others and the environment; and
- Value the integration between research and practice, humanistic research and importance of plurality of methods.

Skill Objectives

The skill objectives may be in the following areas:

- Self-awareness, self-esteem, creative, critical and positive thinking, emotional health, interpersonal communication and social interactions and relationships;
- Skills in policy analysis and action research;
- Innovations in intervention with the select marginalised group to deal their select issue; and
- Methodology of social work education.

Structure: The MPhil and PhD programmes in social work comprise of the following components:

- Class-work in research methodologies and application of statistics, with specific focus on practice-based research and policy analysis;

- Pre-doctoral/MPhil papers on review of social science theories, methodology and research/dissertation on select issues of a marginalised group and intervention in the Indian situation;
- Skill workshop on methodology of social work education, including curriculum development, teaching-learning and evaluation methods, knowledge development and dissemination and so on; and
- Thesis on development of knowledge in one substantive area of social work practice/policy planning/administration/education/training, or practice innovation.

CURRICULUM DEVELOPMENT OF CLASS-WORK

Class-work in progressive social work education may include the subjects and non-graded curricular seminars and workshops, as discussed below:

Subject Curriculum Design

A commitment to praxis necessitates the reflective practice of teaching behaviours that demonstrate a critical approach and increase one's effectiveness at creating a liberating learning environment. Applied to teaching a subject critically, praxis involves moving between a critical perspective, one's teaching practices, evaluative reflection on the liberating and/or dominating aspects of the teaching, and back again to a critical and liberatory perspective (Boyce, 1996). Thus curriculum development of a subject is not a one-time activity, but an ongoing process.

The components of the curriculum design for a subject may be as follows:

- Level at which it is to be offered,
- Foundational, core or optional subject,
- Number of marks and credit hours,
- Knowledge, attitude and skill objectives,
- Links with other subjects,
- Schedule of contents,
- Methods and tools of teaching and learning,
- Linkage with fieldwork practicum,
- Recommended audio-visual aids and case illustrations,
- Recommended books, journals and articles, and
- Methods of evaluation.

Subjects, which are taught for two hours per week for 15 weeks, carry two credits. At the para-professional level, the students should be required to take six two-credit subjects per semester, whereas at the BSW level, they should be required to take seven two-credit subjects per semester, and at the MSW level, again six two-credit subjects per semester.

Curricular Seminars and Workshops

The curricular non-graded seminars and workshops include the following:

- Fieldwork seminars,
- Research seminars,
- Life skill workshops,
- Social work skill workshops, and
- Rural camp/study tour planning meetings.

Identification of Objectives

Objectives normally refer to an intended and pre-specified outcome of a planned programme of teaching and it is expressed in terms of what it is hoped the student will have learned (Eraut, 1989). These should include (either within the objective or in an associated set of assessment criteria) a description of the kind of performances by which achievement will be judged (Toohey, 1999). The subject's objectives for knowledge, attitude and skills may be identified in the context of the objectives for knowledge, attitude and skills of the total social work education programme. Moreover, the current knowledge, attitude and skill levels of the students may be estimated, depending upon the level of the programme.

Leaving aside technical considerations such as clarity, the justification of an objective is based on two kinds of argument – feasibility and desirability (Bloom and others, cited from Eraut, 1989). Feasibility arguments are normally based on evidence from practice. Desirability arguments are of two main kinds: evidence of expressed preferences and arguments from basic values – the former concerns who thinks an objective is desirable, and the latter concerns why it should be thought desirable (Eraut, 1989).

Selection and Organisation of the Content

The sub-themes for the content of a subject may be identified from the following:

- Theories, concepts and conceptual framework
- Historical and contemporary scenario
- International, national and local context
- Demographics and issues in urban/rural areas

- Structure and processes of systems involved
- Review of relevant development and welfare policies, schemes and laws
- Impact on rights to basic needs and marginalisation of vulnerable groups
- People's movements and NGO initiatives
- Methods, techniques, skills and process of social work interventions

According to Toohey (1999), the different sources for selecting the content of the subject include the following:

- Published educational materials such as textbooks and curriculum documents;
- Information from academics teaching in the field;
- Information on current professional practice; and
- Information from students and recent graduates.

Analysis of the curricula of similar courses at other institutions, as well as of textbooks and recent literature, provides a view on what others involved in teaching the subject think is important. Curriculum documents from other institutions occasionally incite unstinting admiration, but are more likely to prompt questions about the importance given to some topics and the inclusion or non-inclusion of others. A general literature review, as would be undertaken at the beginning of any research project, will also provide a useful starting point for the curriculum team (Toohey, 1999).

The scope of the subject may be determined according to the length of the time allocated. The sequence of the course content may be organised so that the students progress continuously in learning tasks through logical steps. Linkage with fieldwork practicum is essential.

Selection of Methods of Teaching-Learning and Evaluation

Social work education requires knowledge-as-action, knowledge that is contextualised culturally and historically, and is shaped by the interaction between students, teachers and the field. The goal of teacher-student interaction should be the same as that of the worker-client interaction, that is, resource building for independent decision-making. Methods in social work education are, therefore, as important to the learning process as methods in social work practice are to the problem-solving process. In order for the teacher-learner transaction to give the same dynamics to training as the worker-client transaction gives to practice, the educator should be a facilitator of learning rather than merely a transmitter of knowledge (Hokenstad and Rigby, 1977).

The specific methods and tools for teaching-learning and evaluation may be selected for teaching a subject or a topic, appropriate to the objectives of the subject/topic. The details of the methods and tools of teaching-learning and evaluation are provided in the chapter on "Methodology of Teaching-Learning and Evaluation".

CURRICULUM DEVELOPMENT OF FIELDWORK PRACTICUM

Objectives of Fieldwork Practicum

Fieldwork practicum is a closely supervised educational internship in a social work setting that provides planned opportunities to apply theory taught in class-work to actual situations, which, in turn, enhances classroom learning. The curriculum of fieldwork practicum may be developed in coordination with the curriculum development of class-work, both aiming at achieving the objectives of the academic programme. Fieldwork practicum may specifically aim at the following objectives:

- Observation and understanding of the interaction between human behaviour and the social, economic and political systems, systemic marginalisation of vulnerable groups at the micro level, and the alternate viewpoints by different stakeholders, including social workers.
- Development of critical self-awareness about one's attributes, values and sensitivities with reference to the ideology of social justice and human rights and ethical requirements of social work profession, through experience.
- Learning and practice of social work methods and skills of work with individuals and the socio-economic-political systems of family, community, state, corporate sector, mass media and non-profit organisations, democratise them, drawing linkages across them, to prevent and ameliorate social problems; and documentation, monitoring and evaluation of one's social work intervention.

Activities of Fieldwork Practicum

Fieldwork practicum may include the following activities:

- Life skill workshops
- Organisational visits
- Concurrent fieldwork
- Block fieldwork

- Social work skill workshops
- Rural/tribal camp/study tour

According to the UGC Second Review Committee on Social Work Education (1980), concurrent fieldwork has considerable value since the skills and attitudes develop only over a period of time. Block fieldwork may be continued where a specific learning gain is attached to it and it is feasible. The rationale of having block fieldwork at the end of the two years needs to be reviewed. The student might probably see this as a period of disengagement, rather than re-engagement, as it comes towards the end of his learning. It is also difficult for the institution to help the student to stay in a location too far from the institution. Hence, it may be necessary to experiment with block fieldwork in the middle of the academic year between October and December. The remainder of the concurrent fieldwork time should be utilised to follow-up on the activities undertaken during the block fieldwork.

Camps and study tours are seen as valid components of the student's field learning. Institutional visits in the same location, especially as a part of the students' orientation to the field of social work at the point of entry, are also recommended (UGC, 1980).

Experiential Approach in Fieldwork Practicum

The fieldwork practicum needs to use the andragogical or the experiential approach. According to Johnson (1986), experiential learning is based on three assumptions:

1. People learn best when they are personally involved in the learning experience;
2. Knowledge has to be discovered if it is to mean anything or make a difference in behaviour; and

3. Commitment to learning is highest when people are free to set their own learning goals and actively pursue them within a given framework.

Johnson (1986) suggests a four-stage cycle in experiential learning:

1. Concrete personal experiences are followed by
2. observation of, reflection on, and examination of one's experiences, which leads to
3. formulation of abstract concepts and generalisations, which leads to
4. hypotheses to be tested in future action.

Thus, experiential learning through fieldwork practicum, results in personal theories about effective intervention and continuously recurs as a person tests out and confirms or modifies his or her personal theories (Johnson, 1986).

Field Instruction

Field instruction comprises of the following roles of the fieldwork practicum supervisor/coordinator:

- Selection and preparation of the setting
- Planning learning experiences/activities
- Guiding fieldwork records
- Conducting individual and group discussions/ conferences
- Developing and using teaching and learning tools
- Evaluation of students and the fieldwork setting

According to the Second Review Committee on Social Work Education (UGC, 1980), it is necessary to evaluate the suitability of fieldwork experience that traditional agency placements provide and to devise other means of learning administrative decisions. Placements selected and the tasks assigned to the students must have significance for the students. Adequate fieldwork opportunities should be made available.

CURRICULUM DEVELOPMENT OF PROJECT REPORT

When education of social work research is modelled on pure social research, it can tell one the state of things as they are, rather than research that helps intervention. In this system, social work students fail to see a direct link between research and practice. As a result of such training, most of the social workers think that they have nothing to do with research. Such training makes social workers poor researchers and poor users of research in the practice situation. This explains why practitioners generally do not document their own work and analyse it. As a result, much of the contributions of social work practitioners to theory building remain irretrievable for the purpose of social work education.

Powers, Meenaghan and Toomey (1985) highlight the need for a practitioner to make informed decisions. These decisions and subsequent practice behaviours are precisely the types of things that professionals should justify. They stressed that the ultimate test of effective knowledge building in any profession is the degree to which the body of knowledge is prescriptive. The emphasis in social work education should be on integration of practice and research towards the development of praxis. The practice methods taught should be research-based and the research course should be practice-based. The research project should be linked with the fieldwork practicum.

A project report may be required in social work education. At the BSW level, its objective may be to learn to document the fieldwork problem, the process of intervention and the outcome, and link these to theories. At the MSW level, the basic/core social work subject on social work research may be coordinated with the project report, the objectives of which may be the following:

Knowledge Objectives

- The range of modern and post-modern ideologies of knowledge;
- Quantitative and qualitative research methodologies that guide social work practice; and
- Exploratory and confirmatory designs for use in social work research.

Attitude Objectives

- Research to be considered an integral part of practice;
- Social work research should study social work practice so that social realities can be improved;
- Social work research facilitates accountability of social work practitioners and voluntary organisations to the people they work with, the sponsors and the society at large;
- People whose lives are being studied should be considered co-researchers; and
- Plurality of methods is necessary for understanding social issues holistically.

Skill Objectives

- Skill to identify the type of research needed according to the stage of practice;
- Skill to carry out literature review and prepare a research proposal;
- Skill to use the participatory approach with plurality of methods; and
- Skill to write the report of the research findings and draw implications for policy planning, practice and further research.

For more details on social work research, see the chapter on "Methodology of Progressive Social Work Research".

CURRICULUM DEVELOPMENT OF CO-CURRICULAR ACTIVITIES

The co-curricular non-graded activities in progressive social work education may include use of library and computers and the following workshops:

- Study skills such as skills for use of the library and the Internet, writing assignments, use of computer and class presentations;
- Skills for professional advancement, that is, skills for preparing resumes, identifying jobs and preparing applications, identifying avenues for higher studies and preparing applications, preparing for job interviews and group discussions, preparing project proposals, and so on; and
- Remedial coaching.

DEVELOPMENT OF A SYSTEM FOR CURRICULUM REVIEW

Progressive social work curriculum needs to be regularly reviewed for its relevance. Annual curriculum review needs to be carried out in the following manner:

- Students may be asked to evaluate the content, the method and the teacher for each subject, each activity of the fieldwork practicum, the project report and the curricular and co-curricular seminars and reports by filling up a questionnaire, which may be partly structured and partly unstructured.
- After each term/semester, groups of educators teaching related subjects may review their subjects together.
- All the students and the faculty members may orally review the whole curriculum at the end of the year and revise it.
- Agency fieldwork instructors and other practitioners may be invited annually to give feedback on the developments in the field, which need accentuation in the class.
- Each social work subject may be annually reviewed and revised based on reflections, new reading and new understanding gained by the teacher, and written and oral feedback from students.

Chapter 4

Methodology of Teaching-Learning and Evaluation in Progressive Social Work Education

INTRODUCTION

The methodology of teaching needs to be viewed as a teaching-learning process, which is based on the ideologies, ethics and mission, the objectives and the curriculum design of the discipline. Progressive social work education requires knowledge-as-action – knowledge that is contextualised culturally and historically, and is shaped by the interaction between students, teachers and the field. The goal of teacher-student interaction should be the same as that of the worker-client interaction, that is, resource building for independent decision-making. Methods in social work education and training are, therefore, as important to the learning process as methods in social work practice are to the problem-solving process. In order for the teacher-learner transaction to give the same dynamics to training as the worker-client transaction gives to practice, the educator should be a facilitator of learning, rather than merely a transmitter of knowledge (Hokenstad and Rigby, 1977).

According to the critical pedagogical ideology, the educator is not the pre-eminent possessor of knowledge. Learners also bring their own interpretative powers to life experiences. Both are co-sharers in the creation of what is known. When no particular interpretation deserves to have a privileged status, then the intellectual skill of critique is essential. Students must learn how to approach whatever content is presented with means for critically assessing its virtues and shortcomings. To prepare students as reflective practitioners, there is a need for expanded ways for them to appreciate their own wisdom and creativity (Weick, 1994).

The process of liberatory education, which is dialogical, affirms the mutual and co-equal roles of teachers and learners and, therefore, appropriate for social work education and training. The dialogical approach to learning is characterised by cooperation and acceptance of inter-changeability and mutuality in the roles of teacher and learner, demanding an atmosphere of mutual acceptance and trust. In this method, all teach and all learn. Without dialogue, there is no communication, and without communication there can be no liberatory education (Heany, 1995).

The methodology of teaching-learning and evaluation in progressive social work education may include the following components:

- Theories and stages of learning,
- Skills, methods and tools of teaching-learning, and
- Methods of evaluation.

THEORIES AND STAGES OF LEARNING

Theories of Learning

Principles of Learning

Learning principles, according to Wheeler (1967), are the following:

- Learning is an active process in which the learner must be involved.
- Learning is affected by individual goals, values and motives.
- Behaviour is a function of the learner's perception.
- Similar situations may elicit different reactions from different learners.
- Group atmosphere affects both learning product and accrued satisfaction.
- All learning is multiple. Though focus may be on one particular learning, other learning takes place simultaneously.

The following are principles of learning according to Lowman (1984):

- It is better for college students to be active seekers than passive recipients of learning.
- For students to be fully engaged in learning, their attention must be focused on the material.
- Differences in intellectual ability among college students will influence their speed of learning; these differences will be more noticeable when the information to be learned is abstract and complex than when it is simple and concrete.

- Students increase their effort if rewarded rather than punished; however, students differ in the teacher behaviours that they find rewarding.
- Students learn and remember information better if they have many cognitive associations to it; learning of isolated information is more difficult and less permanent than learning of information that is connected to a network of other material.
- It is difficult to learn ideas that are very similar unless the differences between them are emphasised. Conversely, it is easier to learn disparate ideas if their similarities are emphasised.
- Students learn images as well as words, and images are more easily remembered, especially if they are vivid and emotionally tinged.
- Students enter every class with positive and negative emotional attitudes that can interfere with learning or can increase motivation and provide an associational network for new learning.
- A moderate amount of anxiety or challenge activates most students and increases learning; however, excessive anxiety interferes with learning.

Additional learning principles, according to the Lions Quest Skills (n.d.), are the following:

- Learners are more receptive to learning when they know its purpose.
- Discussions and activities help linking new information to prior knowledge
- Learning is influenced by the developmental stage of the learners.

Conditions of Learning

According to *A Manual for Participatory Training Methods in Development* (1998), the following are necessary conditions for learning:

- Learners learn when they feel they are personally involved with others in a learning process.
- A climate of respect is developed when a high value is placed on individuals and a sense of caring prevails.
- A climate of acceptance is necessary where learners can be themselves and express their beliefs without fear.
- A climate of openness is necessary when personal concerns, feelings, ideas and beliefs can be expressed and examined openly.
- It is necessary that each individual knows that his/her values, beliefs, feelings and views are important and significant.
- An atmosphere of trust, when people have a feeling of trust in them and in others, helps learning.
- A climate is necessary where differences in people are as acceptable as differences in ideas.
- Learning is facilitated when error is accepted as a natural part of the learning process.
- It helps when alternative solutions can be explored without the pressures of having to find an immediate single answer.

Stages of Teaching-Learning Process

The following are stages of teaching-learning according to Percival and Ellington (1984):

1. Recognition of student's current knowledge level as valuable and bringing it to the fore through their participation.
2. Provide knowledge, its analysis, and self-learning experiences to facilitate comprehension.
3. Encourage participation for relating new knowledge to current knowledge through evaluation.
4. Synthesis will lead to application.

Types of Students

The following is a typology of students according to Lowman (1984):

Compliant Students

- Teacher dependent
- Prefer lectures to discussions
- Conventional
- Lack independence or creativity
- Highly task-oriented
- Do moderately well in examinations

Anxious-Dependent Students

- Teacher dependent
- Excessive concern about grades
- Conventional
- Do moderately well in examinations
- Lack self-confidence

Discouraged Students

- Fatalistic attitude

Independent Students

- Pursue their own goals independently
- Do very well in examinations
- Prefer seminar to lecture classes

Heroes

- Resemble independent students
- Fail to deliver
- Anxious to impress
- Sometimes hostile towards the teacher

Attention-Seeking Students

- Good socialisers
- Intelligent but not intellectual
- Socio-emotional leaders
- Do not perform well in examinations

Silent Students

- Easily ignorable

SKILLS, METHODS AND TOOLS OF TEACHING-LEARNING

Teaching Skills

Teaching skills of creating intellectual excitement, interpersonal rapport and teaching critical thinking skills are necessary for effective learning, as discussed below:

Intellectual Excitement

According to Lowman (1984), an intellectually excited teacher is expected to do the following:

- All content is extremely well organised and presented in clear language.
- Relationships among specific concepts and applications to new situations are stressed.
- Content is presented in an engaging way, with high energy and strong sense of dramatic tension.
- Teacher appears to love presenting the material.

Interpersonal Rapport

Lowman (1984) stated that teachers judged high on interpersonal rapport are extremely warm and open, highly student-centred and predictable as follows:

- Teacher appears to have strong interest in the students as individuals and high sensitivity to subtle messages from them about the way they feel about the material or its presentation.
- Teacher acknowledges students' feelings about matters of class assignments or policy and encourages them to express such feelings.
- Teacher encourages students to ask questions and seems eager for them to express personal viewpoints.
- Teacher communicates both openly and subtly that each student's understanding of the material is important to him or her.
- Teacher encourages students to be creative and independent in dealing with the material, to formulate their own views.

- Teacher obtains regular feedback from students.
- Teacher gives students choices about a few decisions of much smaller consequence – choices between options that are consistent with the objectives and availability of time.

Teaching of Critical Thinking Skills

According to Gibbs and Gambrill (1999), critical thinking involves the careful examination of beliefs and actions. It requires paying attention to the process of reasoning, not just the product. According to them, the following teaching practices promote critical thinking skills in students:

- Present arguments for and against controversial issues presented in class.
- Show students the specific steps that were followed to draw important conclusions in the course.
- Identify underlying assumptions related to conclusions.
- Regularly refer to documentation to support conclusions.
- Teach students how to pose clear questions for themselves.
- Emphasise the value of finding out what is true rather than how to 'win' an argument.
- Reward students for coming to their own well-reasoned conclusions, rather than simply rewarding them for agreeing.
- Give assignments that emphasise how to think through things for oneself rather than memorisation.

According to Orlosky and Smith (1978), the levels of knowledge objectives range from the level of recall and recognition, through comprehension (translation, interpretation and extrapolation), generalisation, analysis (of elements, relationships and organisational principles) and synthesis and up to the level of evaluation, so that one can judge the value of the knowledge in realising specific objectives.

As far as the affective objectives are concerned, they have identified the levels ranging from awareness (receiving stimuli and passively or actively attending to it); to acquiescence (responding to it on request, willingly responding and taking satisfaction in responding); to acceptance of a value (voluntarily responding and seeking out further ways to take part in what is going on); to organisation of the value system; to the highest level of acceptance of a value system (characterisation of oneself).

Methods and Tools of Teaching

Presented below is the Edgar Dale's Cone of Experience (1969, cited from www.work-learning.com/chigraph.htm) that moves from the experience of reading, hearing and seeing abstract information to directly experiencing concrete skills and attitudes, suggesting increased likelihood of learning:

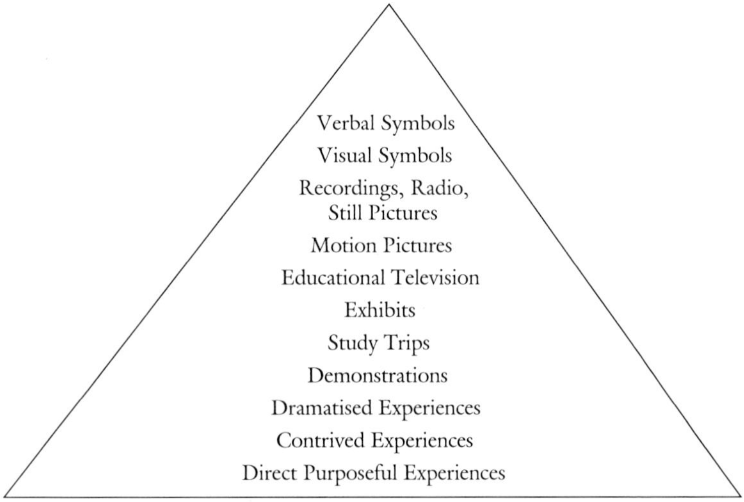

The cone indicates the importance of audio-visual aids and experiential methods of teaching for learning purpose. Thus, lecture is not the best or the only method of teaching. There is a range of methods of teaching providing different learning experiences and the method to be selected for teaching a subject or a topic should be appropriate to the objectives of the subject/topic, as suggested below:

- Knowledge-focused subjects/topics may be taught through lecture and library study and written assignment methods.
- Attitude-focused subjects/topics may be taught through self-study exercises, games or assignments.
- Skill-based subjects/topics may be taught through role-play and other simulation games, case study, field observations and practice.

All the methods need to be followed by self-reflection and discussion.

Methods of Teaching

Lecture Method

Lectures are good for validating information from a respected source (www.fsu.edu/~ids/fac2002/lecture.htm). According to Lowman (1984), following are essentials of the lecture method:

- Fit the material you present to the time you have available.
- Seek concise ways to present and illustrate content. Express concepts in the simplest terms possible and define technical terms when using them.

- Begin each course and class by pricking the students' interest, expressing positive expectations, and sharing the objectives you have for them.
- Follow a prepared outline but include improvised material or illustrations. Appear spontaneous even when you are following the outline closely.
- Break up the monotony of lectures by varying the methods of presentation.
- Use a wide range of voices, gestures and physical movements, but be yourself. Develop a varied and interesting style consistent with your values and personality.
- Give students regular places to catch their breath and ask questions.
- End each lecture with a conclusion that connects what has happened today with what will be covered during the next meeting.
- Be guided by your students during your lectures. Continually observe their reactions, acknowledge them, and modify your approach when indicated.
- Remember in your relationships with students that all of you are persons first, students and teacher second.

Role-Plays and Simulations

The following description of the role-play method is taken from *A Manual for Participatory Training Methods in Development* (1998). This method is used in the following ways:

- Role-play is used to stimulate discussion on complex issues. A brief enactment by trainers or students or both can be used to stimulate further group discussion on similar issues and experiences that students share. The scripting can be done completely or partly by the organisers or totally left to the participants.

- Role-play is a useful method to practice skills. The prime method of learning here is by practising and receiving feedback from students and trainers after the practice. The teacher may demonstrate skills by first acting out the general mistakes that we make and then doing it in the right way. The first demonstration of the right skill may be done at the normal speed. The second time it may be done slowly, stating the key points at each step. Demonstration by the teacher should be followed by practice by the students, under supervision. Simulations are mock-ups of the real thing that include role-plays with props (Kroehnert, 1995).
- A role-play can also be used for a re-enactment of past experiences. In this sense, all students are involved to enact an issue or a situation about which they are familiar in their past. Since all the students share this experience and all of them are involved in re-enactment, learning occurs here through the twin steps of preparation and re-enactment.

In whichever way role-play is used, real consolidation of learning through role-play occurs through the steps of preparation, re-enactment, discussion, processing and analysis with generalization to real life situation.

Case Study

According to *A Manual for Participatory Training Methods in Development* (1998), in the case study method, others' experiences are provided to the group in the form of a case study. These experiences are reflected upon and analysed by the students to then extract or arrive upon new principles. The students' own experiences, values and feelings form the basis for analysing others' experiences. Case studies may be presented in written or verbal forms or even through the medium of film or song, depending upon cultural appropriateness. After presenting the case study, the students may be divided into small groups and given questions to reflect and discuss.

The case study method can be used to convey complex theoretical concepts in a simple way. It allows the group to reflect on its appropriateness in their milieu/life, allows discussions/sharing on potentially threatening situations, on which the students will not be willing to share if asked directly, sharpens students' analytical and diagnostic skills, exposes them to situations they might not ordinarily experience in their own lives, exposes them to similar experiences elsewhere to enable them feel a sense of solidarity and validation and helps in creating new knowledge through collective reflection, analysis and synthesis.

Besides case studies, relevant songs, stories/local folk tales/popular movies/television serials may also be identified, and used to discuss the issues on the agenda.

Assignments

Written assignments may be on analysis of a topic, book review, case analysis, proposal of a field project/research, report of a field visit/field project/research and so on. These assignments require students to research and synthesise information, develop an argument and provide evidence for their judgments. Case study or problem-centred assignments require a performance closer to professional practice. A field project may include applications of knowledge and skills in the field.

Students may be asked to reflect and write on self with reference to human development, family dynamics, attitudes to an issue and so on.

Class presentation of an assignment is a method of learning by sharing. It gives the students a choice to learn more than what can be taught in the limited amount of time the teacher can spend with them. It gives scope for active participation and creativity. The student, who is presenting the assignment, takes up the role of the expert on the selected topic. He or she does the homework in consultation with the teacher and is responsible for the productive use of the time of all the classmates/participants. It is, therefore, important for the student to do the following:

1. Prepare for the presentation enthusiastically
2. Cover the topic comprehensively
3. Cover the topic accurately
4. Prepare to make the presentation interesting
5. Plan to keep the time limits

Discussions

The ORID method, developed by the Institute of Cultural Affairs (1991a), recommends discussion in the following order:

1. O: Objective focus on what they saw/heard (getting the facts).
2. R: Reflection on what feelings were aroused (emotions, feelings, associations).
3. I: Interpretation of it (values, meaning, purpose).

4. D: Decision on what one wants to therefore do (future resolves).

Lowman (1984) described the utility of the discussion method as follows:

Course content: Though not effective for presenting content *per se*, discussion does aid its mastery by encouraging students to actively process what they learn as they sit in class. Asking students to think and a few to speak out loud encourages all students to think more fully about content. Discussion helps students assimilate and integrate information they have initially acquired from readings or lectures. Students can also be asked in discussion to compare and contrast different concepts. Focusing on the similarities and differences that always exist between specific ideas helps to link the ideas in an associational network. Such networks are remembered far longer than isolated concepts. Discussion is useful for emphasising the connections between new and old knowledge.

Thinking skills: Discussion is most useful to teach the process of learning, that is, thinking. Thinking is also stimulated in those who merely listen to their classmates and consider what they might have said themselves. Students learn to approach a problem or topic rationally, monitor their own thinking processes, and question their implicit assumptions.

Attitudes: Discussion is particularly good at revealing students' attitudes. Whether they participate in the discussion or not, students become more aware of their own attitudes and values by comparing them with the values and attitudes expressed by others. Exposure to different views can lead some students to question or even change their implicit assumptions. When students have strong and differing opinions about course concepts, it is relatively easy for a college teacher to bring these out in discussion.

Student involvement: In addition to clarifying content, teaching rational thinking and highlighting affective judgements, discussion is particularly effective at increasing student involvement in classes. However, a discussion leader who lets students talk on and on with little control or direction will soon lose the group's attention.

Interpersonal objectives: Discussion can promote student rapport, independence and motivation. Motivation to learn is increased because students want to work for an instructor who values their ideas and encourages them to be independent. An instructor, who by discussion asks for students' opinions, communicates that he or she cares about their reactions to the course.

The Lions Quest Skills (n.d.) have listed the following tips for leading effective discussions:

- Ask the question and direct participants to think about or write their ideas rather than raise their hands. After a few seconds, call for responses.
- Address the question to the group, not to a specific student. Allow time for all participants to think before calling on someone to share.
- Some of the things participants say will be surprisingly insightful; others will seem frivolous. But, when participants express an idea that is important to them, take them seriously. Otherwise, they may not feel comfortable sharing.
- Accept multiple answers where appropriate, but correct misinformation.
- Do not accept rudeness or inappropriate responses.

- Avoid using more "air time" than participants, during a discussion.
- If you stop discussions after only one student has responded, participants get the impression there was only one right answer to the question.
- Draw shy participants out by occasionally calling on them by name. They still have the right to pass, but showing special interest in them builds self-confidence.

Introduction of a Topic

Smith and Delahaye (1987) recommend the following activities while introducing a topic:

- Explain the topic title and relate it to their current relevant knowledge. If there has been a previous relevant session, review that session.
- Provide an overview of the topic, telling the students what ground they will cover in the session, provide a target, establish appropriate expectations about the content of the session, and allow the group to check progress for themselves.
- Create interest in the session with the help of a joke, a cartoon, and a graph on the overhead projector, a controversial statement, a story of common interest, or a startling question.
- Ask a few questions to know the quantity and quality of the students' knowledge so that you can pitch your presentation at the right level.

Conclusion of a Topic

Smith and Delahaye (1987) recommend the following activities while concluding a theme/topic:

Recapitulate: Briefly go over the main items of the topic. Bring all the pieces together and tie up loose ends. Stress important or key points. The teacher should highlight whatever the students miss out.

Clarify: Allow time for questions to clear up any misunderstandings or problems.

Link: Draw links to subsequent sessions.

Finish: Make sure that students leave the subject with a sense of completion and achievement.

Tools for Teaching

The audio-visual aids useful for teaching-learning include verbal and visual symbols on blackboards, flip charts, charts, posters, flash cards and handouts; newspaper/magazine cuttings; radios and tape recorders; slide shows; and video films, selected according to the objectives of the topics. Tools for teaching also include exercises/games, field illustrations, case studies and so on. Use of these tools should always be followed by discussion.

Handouts

Many college teachers distribute handouts – such as lecture outlines, listings of definitions or formulas, or diagrams. Since the teacher himself/herself prepares them, they are more accurate than what some students would record in their notes. Little time is required to produce handouts, so they are cost-effective. Handouts are a reminder of what the students heard in the lecture. They are no substitute for a clear and engaging lecture from which a student actively creates a personal set of notes (Lowman, 1984).

Blackboards and Flipcharts

Blackboards are a universal feature of classrooms that are easily taken for granted. The act of writing on the blackboard focuses student attention on the lecture. Many excellent teachers routinely write an outline of the day's lecture in one corner of the blackboard before class begins. This provides a useful preview of what is to come (Lowman, 1984).

Flipcharts of newsprint are another popular method of accomplishing the same ends. They allow different coloured marking pens to be used (coloured chalk is difficult to read), and the notes need not be erased during or after class (Lowman, 1984). Flipcharts are often used for brainstorming, recording and reviewing key points from learners and responding to queries. Sheets from flipcharts can also be displayed like posters following the discussion (Gough, 1997).

Electronic Aids

Lowman (1984) discussed the following electronic aids:

- *Overhead transparencies* are the most commonly used electronic aid because they are so easy to prepare. Many teachers routinely employ them in place of the blackboard, using photocopy machines to transfer material to transparencies before class or writing directly on the transparencies with specially designed pens.
- *Slides* are much more difficult for most teachers because support personnel must photograph materials and develop film, but their visual quality is superior to that of transparencies. When the course content requires photographs of important objects or scenes (paintings,

buildings, villages, geological features), 35 mm slides are indispensable.

- *Audiotape and videotape cassettes* have many of the advantages of motion pictures, although television screen sizes severely limit the number of students to whom they can be shown effectively. Modern video projectors are a decided improvement over standard monitors. Cassettes have the advantage of allowing the instructor to show desired segments easily.

METHODS OF EVALUATION

Students need to be evaluated with reference to the extent to which the learner objectives of integration of the knowledge, attitude and skill areas are met. According to the UGC regulations (2003) regarding the minimum standards of instruction through formal education, the final or the semester-end or the year-end examination should not be the only method of evaluation. It states that "there shall be continuous sessional evaluation in each course in addition to trimester/semester/ year-end examinations". As Rajput (n.d.) states, the annual examination system has not only reduced the quality of teaching, it has also bred corruption and a lot of social tension. This problem has been identified way back in 1902 when the Indian University Commission observed: "the greatest evil from which the university education in India suffers is that teaching is subordinate to examinations."

In 1959, the University Education Commission, headed by Dr. Sarvepalli Radhakrishnan, remarked: "If we have to suggest one single reform in university education, it would be that of examination." The National Policy on Education, 1986 prescribed that the examination system should be recast so as to ensure a method of assessment that is a valid and reliable measure of student development. The predominance of external examinations should be reduced, by streamlining the evaluation machinery at the institutional level. However, the emphasis on final examination and external examinations in higher education in India continues.

This section discusses the range of methods of evaluation with reference to their use and criteria for their selection. It also discusses the system of grading and the internal/external evaluation.

Use of Evaluation Methods

Toohey (1999) describes the different written and oral methods of evaluation and their use, as follows:

Written Evaluation

- Objective-type tests, including multiple choice, true/false and short answers, are most useful for testing knowledge and understanding.
- Essay-type examinations and evaluations are more appropriate for testing higher levels of thinking and more complex intellectual performances. Essay assignments require students to research and synthesise information, develop an argument and provide evidence for their judgements.
- Open-book examinations must be designed to test problem-solving and the application and interpretation of knowledge, rather than students' ability to look up the right answer.
- Case study or problem-centred examinations and assignments require a performance closer to professional practice.

- Practical/professional tasks may include straightforward applications of knowledge and skills.
- Reflective tasks include professional journals, diaries and logs, together with reflective essays and autobiographies. They are used to assess reflection on practice, growth in understanding, reasoning behind judgements and actions, and the development of professional attitudes. Although students often find journals unfamiliar and difficult, they do force most students to think more deeply about practical exercises and field placements, and may help to integrate theory and practice. Because it is difficult to specify performance standards for professional journals, they are often assessed on a 'satisfactory/unsatisfactory' basis.

Oral Evaluation

Oral evaluations usually take the form of seminar presentations, project presentations, oral examinations or vivas, and sometimes the evaluation of class participation.

- Oral presentations and seminars, based on written assignments, can provide a way of assessing students' ability to research and organise information and develop an argument. More interesting is likely to be the student's ability in making an oral presentation and leading a discussion – aspects in which students often receive little or no preparation.
- Evaluation of class participation, usually justified on the grounds that it improves preparation, attendance and the quality of discussion, is even more problematic. Here, the teacher must assess not one but many performances at the

same time, and the criteria for successful performance are often unclear to all parties.

- Oral examinations and vivas are most likely to be useful as a follow-up to the evaluation of a practical or professional task. Here, they can be used to check the reasoning behind actions and judgements, and to see whether the student can reason from a particular context to other cases. Because oral examination stand to be less reliable than written forms of evaluation, they should not be used for testing knowledge which could just as easily be tested in written form, unless there is some factor which makes writing difficult, such as student disability.

Criteria for Selection of Method of Evaluation

According to Toohey (1999), selection of the method of evaluation, system of grading and internal/external assessor may be made, depending upon the following criteria:

- The extent to which the evaluation reflects the learning goals of the course, that is the validity of the evaluation.
- The extent to which the results of the evaluation can be trusted, that is the reliability of the evaluation.
- The extent to which the evaluation supports and promotes real learning. The demands of evaluation are a key factor in pushing students towards a surface approach to learning.
- The cost of the methods chosen.

System of Grading

Research findings show that the greater the number of performance levels that the marking scheme attempts to distinguish, the less reliability there is likely to be among markers (Toohey,

1999). The award of marks also does not take into consideration varying standards of question papers in different subjects. As marks in different subjects are based on different scales and measure different attributes, the total marks (aggregates) do not indicate an overall index of a student's level of performance. Classifying on aggregate marks is, therefore, unscientific. Grades, on the other hand, classify students into "ranges" instead of "points" thereby reducing the error of judgement. It is argued that use of grades would eliminate anomalies of the marking system because a grading system just shows relative positions, instead of absolute standards attained by students. Grades, therefore, provide a more meaningful profile of achievement levels (IQRA, 2002).

According to Toohey (1999), the grading system used in most universities and colleges requires that the work to be evaluated is given a numerical mark, that marks for all pieces of work are combined into a percentage and that a grade classification is then allocated using either a letter grade (A-F) or categories such as 'fail', 'pass', 'credit', 'distinction', or 'high distinction'. Grades are often expected to fall into a pattern approaching a 'normal' distribution and may be adjusted to ensure that they do so. That is, the system in use is basically norm-referenced. Rather, it is a code for a qualitative judgement, which might have more meaning for all concerned if it were expressed in words (Toohey, 1999).

The University Grants Commission's report on *Examinations Reform: A Plan of Action* (1973) recommended the introduction of the grading system with a seven-point scale: O = Outstanding (6), A = Very Good (5), B = Good (4), C = Average (3), D = Below Average (2), E = Poor (1), and F = Very Poor (0).

According to Toohey (1999), more important than precise ranking of students is achieving a clearer understanding among students, markets and the community about what different grade levels signify. He provides the following interpretations of the grades:

- The 'A' grade performance requires students to show a thorough understanding of the concepts that they have been taught but also to be able to use the concepts and ideas beyond the immediate applications they may have studied. It is characterised by a high level of abstract thinking, which enables students to generalise to new contexts, make applications or draw conclusions that are apparently original.
- For a 'B' grade, students need to show that they have a clear understanding of the major concepts and ability to see applications – that they can understand the question, put up a good argument, and show judgement about what is important and what is less important.
- The 'C' class performances show understanding of most of the concepts dealt with, but little evidence of integration. Students have not been able to relate all aspects in a coherent whole, or think through all of the implications of specific applications. However, there is evidence of some understanding, coverage and effort.
- Performances at the 'D' level show some understanding of one or a few basic aspects of the topic. There are some serious problems with the work, but to fail it would be too drastic. Re-submission may be required.
- The 'F' (failing) grade is reserved for irrelevant, incomplete or plagiarised responses.

Internal/External Evaluation

Internal or external evaluation is a decision to be made that will effect the validity and reliability issues as well as the cost. Convincing arguments have been made in the educational literature for the value of involving students in the evaluation process in order to assist them in taking responsibility for their own learning – as they will need to do after graduation (Toohey, 1999).

The teaching-learning and evaluation methodology for progressive training programmes is discussed in the next chapter.

CHAPTER 5

Methodology of Progressive Training Programmes

INTRODUCTION

Social work educators need to know the methodology of progressive training programmes in order to conduct the following:

- Skill workshops for social work students;
- Continuing education programmes for social work practitioners and educators; and
- Extension education programmes.

The experiential and participatory training methodology is at the core of training programmes.

Experiential Learning

According to Johnson (1986), experiential learning is based on three assumptions as under:

1. People learn best when they are personally involved in the learning experience;

2. Knowledge has to be discovered if it is to mean anything or make a difference in behaviour; and
3. Commitment to learning is highest when people are free to set their own learning goals and actively pursue them within a given framework.

Johnson (1986) suggests a four-stage cycle in experiential learning:

1. Concrete personal experiences are followed by,
2. observation of, reflection on, and examination of one's experiences, which leads to,
3. the formulation of abstract concepts and generalisations, which leads to,
4. hypotheses to be tested in future action.

Thus, experiential learning results in personal theories about effective behaviour and continuously recurs as a person tests out and confirms or modifies his or her personal theories (Johnson, 1986).

Participatory Methodology

In the participatory methodology, it is assumed that knowledge and education are never neutral and the trainer's role is to help the participants understand where their own views have come from, to challenge pre-conceptions and to encourage them to consider other possibilities. It assumes that society can be transformed by the engagement of critically conscious persons, through a process of deconstruction, reconstruction and transformation. Participants' life experiences are the major source of knowledge in this method. The trainers are not teachers, but facilitators, and partners with the participants in this process of social change.

TRAINING METHODS

A combination of the following participatory and experiential methods may be planned to meet different topics/objectives of training and vary pace and rhythm:

- Lecturette (small lecture) by facilitator
- Lecture by guest speaker
- Self-reflection and expression
- Pairing and sharing, small and large group activities
- Brainstorming and rounds
- Workshops
- Role-plays and simulations and case studies
- Games and exercises
- Assignments
- Training tools
- Field visits
- Discussions to follow all these methods

Use of Role-plays and simulations, training tools, case study and discussions have already been discussed in the section on methods of teaching in the chapter on "Methodology of Teaching-Learning and Evaluation". Other methods are described below:

Lecturette and Lecture

The facilitator may provide small lectures or lecturettes to introduce the theme or the sub-themes. A guest speaker may be invited for lectures on specialised subjects.

Pairing and Sharing, Small and Large Group Activities

Pairing helps the group members to reflect and share with a partner. It may be done between participants sitting next to each other, making sure that everyone is covered.

Small groups are very useful for several tasks, such as discussion of specific aspects of the topic through case studies, situations or newspaper/magazine cuttings, creative work and preparing role-plays, for presentation to the large group. In small group activities, participants learn from being part of a developing team, which carries out many tasks and activities during the programme. It is particularly useful when the subject of the programme relates closely to interpersonal skills or team working. Six to eight is an ideal size of a small group, the exact size may depend upon the task. The simplest way to form groups is to number the participants serially, according to the number of the small groups to be formed. Small groups may be formed afresh for every task so that there are no permanent small groups (Staley, 1982).

In large group activities such as brainstorming, rounds, games, exercises, songs and energisers, all the participants can participate. Other large group activities, such as role-plays and simulations, essay competition, debates, organising awareness campaigns and so on, involve all the members at the level of thinking but only some may participate verbally or behaviourally.

Rounds and Brainstorming

Round is a method by which every participant has an opportunity to say something quickly, in turns, in answer to a question or to report an opinion or feeling. Rounds are useful quick monitoring exercise to give a sense of individual and group learning. It is particularly useful if you have uneven participation in the group (Williams and others, 1994).

Brainstorming is a structured process that encourages the generation of a large quantity of ideas in a group setting. All ideas are recorded, and no judgements or evaluations are made, while recording. These are clarified and discussed later. It fosters creativity by encouraging people to think beyond the conventional and leads to synergy (Rees, 1998).

Workshops

The workshop method is useful for generating creativity and synergy for team consensus in a short amount of time. The Institute of Cultural Affairs (1991b) recommends five steps for the workshop method as described below:

1. ***Setting the stage:*** Setting the stage include highlighting a focus question and outlining the process and timeline.
2. ***Generating new ideas:*** First ask the group to brainstorm individually, and put down their three best ideas. Let them put each idea boldly on a card and send to the facilitator. Read the card aloud and place randomly on the board. Accept and acknowledge all responses. Indicate that there are no wrong answers. Only clarification may be sought from the person who suggests the idea. Ask for any additional ideas.
3. ***Forming new relationships:*** Ask the group to develop clusters of similar ideas displayed.
4. ***Discerning the consensus:*** Discuss each cluster with reference to what it means. Accordingly, give it a title. Border title cards to distinguish them from other cards.
5. ***Confirming the resolve:*** Arrange the clusters according to their relationships to each other. Discuss the steps undertaken, where did the group get most involved, what breakthroughs did the group have, what is the significance of the work done and what are the next steps.

Games and Exercises

A game or an exercise is normally simple and brief, requires all the participants to participate, is relaxing and enjoyable, inexpensive, predictable and adaptable to a variety of situations. The well-known games such as dumb charade, passing the parcel, Chinese whisper and so on can be adapted for the theme. These need to be followed by discussion for the group to see the connection with the theme. The common games/exercises are icebreakers and mid-course energisers.

Icebreakers help in the following ways:

- Allow the participants to introduce themselves to each other in a playful manner;
- Lead into the topic matter, in a relaxed manner and bring the major issue to the fore of the group consciousness; and
- Do on-the-spot assessment of the relevant awareness, attitudes and skills of the participants.

Mid-course energisers are similar in design to the icebreakers but they are meant for groups that know each other and the theme already. The Lions Quest Skills (n.d.) have described energisers as brief activities that can help a group get acquainted, spark a discussion, change the pace, or bring closure to an activity. Here are some other suggestions:

- Begin by briefly describing the activity, its basic rules and purpose.
- Then demonstrate it with some volunteers, adding rules and explanations as you go.
- Play yourself. Be a positive model for fair play and cooperation.
- Allow participants to observe if they choose.

- Adapt activities whenever necessary. Change the rules, materials, boundaries, size of teams, or anything else to make the activity more fun for your classes.
- Talk about the energiser afterward. Point out the cooperative behaviours participants used. Talk about working towards a common goal and helping one another. Ask what they learned, how they solved a problem, or whether the activity turned out differently than they expected.

Assignments

Preparation

Individual and/or group assignments may be planned on different sub-themes of the theme and presented with the help of audio-visual aids. Its preparation includes the following activities:

- Orientation to assignments
- Field visits
- Visit to a documentation centre that is specialised in the theme/sub-themes
- Individual/ group planning
- Library work
- Consultation with faculty guide
- Finalising the assignment and planning its presentation

Presentation

Adequate time may be planned for each presentation on a sub-theme, with the help of audio-visual aids, followed by discussion and inputs by faculty guides.

Self-Reflection and Expression

Self-reflection and expression may be facilitated through diary-keeping, anonymous disclosure, sentence completion, statement ranking, quizzes, guided fantasy or visualisation and creative expressions and homework.

- Diary-keeping is an important method for training programmes as it allows the group members to reflect and to talk to themselves, at the beginning, during or at the end. At the end of a topic, ask the group to write down the following in their diary:
    1. What did you learn from this topic?
    2. What will you do to follow up what you have learnt? Write down two major decisions that you have taken for follow up.
    3. Write down any other thoughts that come to your mind.
- Sentence completion, statement ranking and quizzes stimulate thinking and expression.
- Guided fantasy or visualisation can be used for private reflection and shared with the group. It is useful to start with general relaxation to enable individuals to free their imaginations.
- Creative work includes collage, drawing, painting, modelling, composing songs, poems, stories, or plays. These can be done individually or as a group. It is important to stress that these activities are vehicles for ideas, not a test of people's talents or abilities (Williams and others, 1994).
- Anonymous disclosure allows for individuals to share honest opinions with reference to controversial topics

and for the group to identify the range of opinions on the subject. The individuals should not be sought to own their opinions (Spinks and Clements, 1999).

FACILITATION TECHNIQUES

Besides creating an atmosphere of acceptance, respect and trust that would draw out participation, facilitators need to facilitate the process of self-discovery, in the following ways:

- Combine structure with freedom, so that the group can be trained with maximum flexibility and creativity, within realistic boundaries (Rees, 1998);
- Facilitate learning from the group's life experiences;
- Provide a range of learning experiences and activities;
- Link scientific knowledge to day-to-day experiences;
- Use simple language;
- Maintain continuity and sustained interest from introduction to conclusion and objectives to review; and
- Monitor the group's understanding and involvement with the programme.

Verbal Techniques

According to Rees (1998), following are the verbal techniques used by the facilitators: asking questions, probing, paraphrasing, re-directing questions and comments, referencing back, giving positive reinforcement, including quieter members, encouraging divergent views, summarising and bridging.

Asking Questions

According to Smith and Delahaye (1987), following are useful tips for asking questions and responding to answers:

- Asking questions helps to check reactions and understanding.
- People learn more through feedback than through anything else and it grips their attention.
- Acknowledge initiative, hard work, and answers (even when incorrect).
- When a participant gives an incorrect answer, ensure that the he/she answers it correctly by the end of the session.
- Look for non-verbal signs of comprehension such as smiles, frowns and nods.
- Provide frequent opportunities for participants to ask questions.
- The participants need to be clear at all times why they are doing what they are doing.
- Map the participants' world, meet them where they are, talk their language and they will listen.
- Give the learners choices.

Following are the do's and don'ts of asking questions according to Smith and Delahaye (1987):

Do's

- Distribute your questions equally among the participants.
- Use easy questions at the start of the session (to get the group used to answering questions successfully)

and for the shy or quiet person (to encourage participation).

- Include questions (fully expressed) in your session plan.
- Re-phrase your question if a participant does not understand it. Try to avoid the temptation to answer the question yourself. You can re-phrase a question with simpler words, relating it more directly to an idea the participant already understands, expanding it with some explanation, or breaking it down into component stages or questions that can be answered sequentially. Alternatively, you could redirect the question to another participant.
- Compliment correct answers.
- If an answer is not completely wrong, identify the part of the answer that is right and reward it.
- Use the direct question for the inattentive person.

Don'ts

- Don't question the group in a regular order (for example, from right to left around the room).
- Don't use long, involved questions. Don't use leading questions. These you can often identify because they can start or end in "don't you?"
- Don't overuse yes/no questions. These give limited response variety and have a 50/50 chance of being answered correctly. You can effectively use a yes/no question to get a "sleeper" involved initially. Then, you can ask the sleeper to justify his or her answer.

- Don't use ambiguous questions. These are questions that are open to different interpretations. They usually generate confusion and/or argument.

The Lions Quest Skills (n.d.) have listed the following tips for leading effective discussions:

- Ask the question and direct participants to think about or write their ideas rather than raise their hands. After a few seconds, call for responses.
- Address the question to the group, not to a specific participant. Allow time for all participants to think before calling on someone to share.
- Some of the things participants say will be surprisingly insightful; others will seem frivolous. But when participants express an idea that is important to them, take them seriously. Otherwise, they may not feel comfortable sharing.
- Accept multiple answers where appropriate, but correct misinformation.
- Do not accept rudeness or inappropriate responses.
- Avoid using more "air time", than participants, during a discussion.
- If you stop discussions after only one participant has responded, participants get the impression there was one right answer to the question. Many "So what?" and "Now what?" questions ask for opinions.
- When groups are newly formed or lack cohesion, ask participants to become more respectful of one another, ask them to share with a partner, small group, and finally the large group.

- Sharing with a partner usually takes less time than large group discussion. Sharing with a partner or small group requires and stimulates a higher energy level from everyone in the room.
- Draw shy participants out by occasionally calling on them by name. They still have the right to pass, but showing special interest in them builds self-confidence.

Probing

According to Rees (1998), probing helps in the following ways:

- Find the root of an issue or problem.
- Enlighten other group members.
- Explore a concern or idea that may otherwise be overlooked.
- Encourage group members to explore issues in greater depth and to value their own thinking process.
- Open the group up to more honest sharing of information and concerns.
- Increase creativity and open-mindedness.

Paraphrasing

Paraphrasing is the act of re-stating what another person has said. Rees (1998) provides the following guidelines for paraphrasing:

- Paraphrase only to check for understanding.
- Do not paraphrase to improve upon the speaker's wording.
- Avoid adding to or changing what the speaker said.

- Paraphrase when a group member is having difficulty expressing ideas more clearly.
- Simply restate what was said when you think other members did not hear the speaker.

Re-directing Questions and Comments

Re-directing invites group members to respond to questions or comments that were directed to the facilitator. The technique encourages dialogue among participants and draws attention away from you. It encourages group members to come up with their own solutions and thoughts as much as possible (Rees, 1998).

Referencing Back

Referencing back is the technique of referring back to something one of the group members said earlier for the purposes of enhancing the discussion and tying group members' ideas to one another. This encourages members to acknowledge and build on one another's ideas. It demonstrates that you are listening to everyone and giving credit to people for his/her comments (Rees, 1998).

Non-Verbal Techniques

The non-verbal techniques used by facilitators are the following: active listening, voice, eye contact, attentiveness, facial expressions, body language, enthusiasm and dress (Rees, 1998).

Group Work Techniques

Group functioning is an important tool for life skills training. Group is a collection of individuals with a reason for being together. Membership in a group may be voluntary or imposed. The life of a group may be long or short (Rees, 1998). Each member brings unique perspectives, talents and skills to the group, which needs to be valued and fostered so that the group diversity flourishes and grows. Therefore, each member should be encouraged to share, no matter how different his or her contributions might be. Every member, in turn, has a responsibility to contribute his or her best for the betterment of the group functioning.

Group Learning

In small group work, participants learn from being part of a developing team, which carries out many tasks and activities during the programme. It is particularly useful when the subject of the training relates closely to interpersonal skills or teamwork. Six to eight is an ideal size of a small group.

According to Mumford (2000), skills of learning in groups are:

- Enabling fellows to share air time appropriately
- Being non-defensive about own actions and learning
- Being supportive about issues/concerns of others
- Being open in initiating and responding to issues
- Listening effectively
- Accepting help
- Being creative in response to problems
- Risk-taking
- Understanding and use learning styles
- Using strength of others as learners
- Helping motivate others as learners

Group Decision-Making

At the heart of group functioning is democratic group decision-making, which is the affirmation of each participant's dignity, worth and welfare. When genuine respect is received from others, each person will feel comfortable in revealing his or her ideas, confident that no one will ridicule or condemn them. Even if a solution is not finally adopted as a solution or plan, the one who offered it still retains dignity and a sense of worth if given a respectful and courteous hearing (Khavari and Khavari, 1989).

In group decision-making, each person should avoid becoming attached to his or her own ideas or preferences. Once expressed, the idea no longer belongs to an individual, but becomes the property of the group, which means that the contributor can then look at the idea just as objectively as the other members. This leaves the group free to accept or reject the idea without fear of hurting the feelings of the one who suggested it. All members should fully understand that rejection of an idea is not a rejection of its originator (Khavari and Khavari, 1989).

According to *A Manual for Participatory Training Methodology in Development* (1998), decision-making within a group takes place in one or more of the following manners:

- *A Plop:* One individual suggests a decision to which there is no response and the decision is adopted by default.
- *Self-Authorised:* The individual who assumes authority makes a decision.
- *Pairing:* Two individuals joining forces make a decision: one floats the idea, the other seconds it and the decision is made on behalf of the group.

- *Minority group:* The clique makes the decision and the rest accept it.
- *Vote:* The decision depends upon the number of people adhering to it.
- *Consensus:* In true consensus, there is open discussion, everyone has contributed to the discussion, all angles have been considered and everyone is in full agreement and is prepared to act on the decision taken.

The group decision-making by consensus requires the following steps:

1. The team members should be relaxed and seated in a circle for the decision-making.
2. Every participant should share what the problem is from their point of view and listen to one another, with the intent to understand.
3. Explore the facts first, with reference to who, where, when, why and how.
4. Discuss feelings, opinions and perceptions attached to these facts and then carry out its analysis.
5. Carry out a brainstorming of suggestions for action without evaluating them. Sometimes, one idea inspires a member to think of a way to make it work better, followed by even a better idea from someone else, creating group synergy.
6. Discuss the suggestions with reference to criteria such as the following:
    - the resources/capacity that the team has to implement each, and
    - the advantages and disadvantages that each may lead to with reference to the team and the individual members.

7. Create a solution that would satisfy all the members and meet the above criteria.
8. Allocate roles to implement the decision taken but make a joint commitment and take joint responsibility for its consequences.
9. Monitor the consequences of implementation of the decision and decide if there is a need to change it. Instead of regretting the decision, take it as a learning experience.
10. Allow the team to make mistakes in decision-making.

Dealing with Lack of Group Participation

Spinks and Clement (1999) state that group participation may be limited due to the need for a comfort zone and avoidance. People prefer to stay in their comfort zones for the following reasons:

- Fear of having one's views attacked or questioned.
- Lack of conformity with accepted or encouraged values.
- Lack of commitment.
- Feeling of risk taking.
- Fear of being misunderstood.
- Lack of knowledge.

Staying-put in the safe, known and familiar comfort zone is certainly one means by which participants avoid having to confront and deal with real and significant issues and problems which impact upon the real world of everyday life. Some of the strategies of avoidance listed by Spinks and Clement (1999) are silence, aggressive/cynical/ridiculing tone or body language of looking away, fidgeting and so on. They point out that the trainers may also tend to avoid the avoidance strategies. Instead, they need to deal with avoidance by noticing, interpreting, addressing, allowing feedback and encouraging involvement, disclosure and risk taking. Use of a confidential question or suggestion box helps the participants to feel comfortable asking or making suggestions they are not comfortable asking openly.

According to the Lions Quest Skills (n.d.) following are the guidelines to facilitate participants to work in groups:

- Model and praise cooperative skills.
- Begin with small groups. The less skilled participants are in group work, the smaller the group should be. As group skills improve, the size of groups can increase.
- Mix groups according to sex, reading ability, language fluency, ethnicity, leadership skills and thinking skills.
- To counter people's natural tendency to stay with their closest friends, have them form pairs and small groups with people they don't know well.
- Clearly explain projects and time limits. Check for understanding by randomly selecting someone to explain the activity.
- Act as a guide and process checker, while trusting the group to solve its own problems.
- Monitor each group to make sure everyone is participating.

Conflict Resolution in Groups

According to the Lions Quest Skills (n.d.), conflicts among participants may be managed as follows:

- Encourage participants to discuss solutions rather than blame others.
- Consistently enforce the ground rules.
- Handle problems quickly and discreetly, training participants with respect and fairness.

- Share reactions to inappropriate behaviours and explain why the behaviours are unacceptable.
- Talk outside of class with participants who continue to disregard the group rules.

Group conflicts may be resolved through the following collaborative steps:

- The group to identify the real issue of conflict and determine to solve the conflict.
- Begin with an attitude of respect for and acceptance of each other.
- Focus on one issue at a time, decide what is the uppermost concern and discuss it.
- Everyone to own one's opinions, feelings and action and not transfer to or label the other.
- Don't start defending yourself.
- Ask questions instead of personal attacks or counter-attacks.
- Everyone to understand other's views with a non-judgemental attitude and be sensitive to other's needs and perceptions, by imagining oneself in their role.
- Maintain a here and now orientation.
- Be specific and realistic about expectations from one another.
- Emphasise points of agreement as a foundation for discussion of points of argument.
- Everyone to put forth one's suggestions to solve the conflict and the group to discuss the pros and cons of each suggestion.

- Avoid a "win-lose" position. The attitude that "I am going to win, and you are going to lose" will more likely result in both losing. If you stay flexible, all can win.
- Develop goals, which are basically compatible.
- Seek solutions rather than deciding who is to blame.
- Work towards a solution most acceptable to the group, irrespective of who made it, or simply agree to disagree.
- Make a commitment to implement the solution and take responsibility for its consequences.
- If one has made a mistake, admit it and if one has hurt others, apologise.
- Learn from the experience.

PLANNING A TRAINING PROGRAMME

One needs to make a commitment to praxis in training programme, which involves moving between preparation and planning, one's programme practices, evaluative reflection on the programme, and back again to fresh preparations and re-planning. Thus, planning for awareness and training programme is not a one-time activity, but an ongoing process.

Plan for a training programme should include the following components:

- Theme
- Need Assessment of the Participants
- Objectives
- Schedule of Topics and Activities
- Resource Persons
- Recommended Reading Material Plan

- Plan for Field Visits
- Planning the Opening Session
- Planning the Closing Session
- Organisational Plan

In spite of a good plan, the facilitator should be flexible to change the plan at the last minute, depending upon the group processes and the emerging needs.

Need Assessment of the Participants

Training programmes should be planned according to the needs of the participants. Needs can be understood with reference to the following factors with the help of an oral or a written assessment:

- Developmental tasks of their age group
- Gender-related needs
- Socio-economic class related needs
- Protection needs of their life situation
- Setting in which they are coming together: schools, colleges, hospitals, health centres, workplaces, clubs and associations, institutions, voluntary organisations and housing societies
- What life skill themes they have already been trained for and current level of the life skills
- Expectations from the programme

Objectives

The objectives of the training programme may be identified based upon the aim of the programme and the need assessment of the participants. Aims serve the crucial function of guiding education, but they cannot be directly observed or evaluated. They are orientations, not specific quantifiable outcomes (Ornstein and Hunkins, 1998).

Objectives normally refer to an intended and pre-specified outcome of a planned programme of teaching and it is expressed in terms of what it is hoped the students will have learned (Eraut, 1989). These should include (either within the objective or in an associated set of assessment criteria) a description of the kind of performances by which achievement will be judged (Toohey, 1999). Leaving aside technical considerations such as clarity, the justification of an objective is based on two kinds of argument – feasibility and desirability (Bloom and others, cited from Eraut, 1989). Feasibility arguments are normally based on evidence from practice. Desirability arguments are of two main kinds: evidence of expressed preferences and arguments from basic values – the former concerns who thinks an objective is desirable, the latter concerns why it should be thought desirable (Eraut, 1989).

Objectives of a training programme should specify the critical awareness components, the value components and the life skill components.

Schedule of Topics and Activities

The theme may be divided into topics, depending on the objectives of the programme. The topics may be selected according to the length of the time allocated. The sequence of the topics may be organised so that the participants progress continuously in learning tasks through logical steps. The schedule may include the topics, the activities, the equipment needed, and the time taken. It should also include time for short and lunch breaks.

Resource Persons

For training social work practitioners and educators, appropriate resource persons may be identified from among applied social scientists, development studies scholars, policy and programme makers or implementers, social work practitioners and educators, functionaries of voluntary organisations and activists of people's movements. As people it helps if they are lively and enthusiastic, organised and punctual, and resourceful with examples and illustrations.

Recommended Reading Material and Audio-Visual Plan

Recommended reading material may be identified on the theme, including relevant theories, concepts, issues, research, United Nations documents, government policies and programmes, interventions by voluntary and international organisations, and classified more or less according to the sub-themes. A bibliography and a list of audio-visuals may be compiled on the theme. The articles, the bibliography and the list of audio-visuals may be photocopied, bound with a page of contents and distributed to the participants.

The recommended books may be displayed separately in the library and the participants may be allowed to read these and other books in the reading hall and issue one book at a time, to be returned before the last day of the programme. A sale and exhibition may also be planned during the training programme for books on the theme.

Planning the Opening Session

The opening session may be planned to include the following formalities:

- Welcome to the group
- Introduction of the trainers and the group participants
- Clarification of the aims
- Confirmation of administrative details
- Icebreaker
- Allocation of tasks
- Sharing expectations and setting ground rules
- Clarification of the objectives
- Introducing the theme

Allocation of Tasks

The following tasks may be daily allocated among the group members, for their active participation in the planning and conducting of the sessions:

- *Seating arrangements:* maintains the circular seating arrangement every day.
- *Maintenance of the blackboard:* keeps the blackboard clean and assists the resource person with writing on it.
- *Creative use of the flannel board:* coordinates use of the flannel boards for display by the course coordinator and the participants.
- *Use of the overhead projector and other audio-visual equipment:* assists the resource person with use of the overhead projector and its screen and other equipment.

- *Coordination of field visits:* coordinates formation of groups by sub-themes and conducting of common field visits.
- *Thanks-giving:* allocates the task of thanks-giving to each Resource person to different participants.
- *Timekeeper:* maintains the time factor with reference to punctuality of the participants and their participation in discussion.
- *Coordination of preparation of daily summaries:* allocates the task of preparation of daily summaries and their presentations either end of the day, or beginning of the next day.

Sharing Expectations and Setting Ground Rules

The group may be asked to share their expectations from the programme and list those on the board as what they 'Want'. Then ask them what they are willing to give to the programme and list these as 'Give'. The 'Give' list should lead to setting of ground rules for the programme. The group may be involved in setting ground rules for group conduct during the programme, including the following, some of which are given by Mumford (2000):

- Enables fellows to share air time appropriately.
- Be non-defensive about own opinions and actions.
- Support issues/concerns of others.
- Be open in initiating and responding to issues.
- Ask questions to elicit information.
- Listen sensitively, without criticising.
- Accept help.
- Be creative in response to problems.

- Use strength of others as learners.
- Motivate others as learners.
- Invite the quiet ones to talk.
- Give positive feedback to others.
- Help the group reach a decision.
- Care about success of other members.
- Maintain confidentiality of personal sharing.

Introducing the Theme

Introducing the theme would include the following activities:

- Defining the key concepts and topics.
- Baseline assessment of the group with respect to the theme.
- Inviting group expectations with reference to the most pressing and relevant issues.
- Clarification of the awareness, attitude and skill objectives.

A theme of training may be initiated with an icebreaker or an audio-visual pertaining to the theme. The icebreaker may be followed by a lecturette on defining the key concepts and topics of the theme. The baseline assessment of the group with respect to the theme may be done through a brief questionnaire or oral question-answers. Group expectations may be written on the flip charts, discussed with reference to which ones are feasible to be covered by the programme and then referred to at the time of evaluation. The introductory session may end with clarification of the awareness, attitude and skill objectives of the programme.

Planning the Closing Session

The closing session should be planned to include summarisation, self-assessment, review and certificate giving.

Self-Assessment

At the end of the training programme, the group may be asked to carry out their self-assessment with reference to their need assessment, by filling up a questionnaire covering the following aspects:

- How do you feel about the training programme?
- What knowledge, attitude and skills did you learn from the programme?
- What was the most important learning for you?
- What will you do to follow up what you have learnt?
- What will be particular useful to you in the real world?
- To what extent did you participate in this programme?
- What contribution did you make to others' learning of this topic?

Review

As discussed in *A Manual for Participatory Training Methodology in Development,* following are the characteristics of participatory evaluation:

- *Shared control:* Both the learners and the trainers maintain shared control over the process of evaluation.
- *Developmental:* It helps in strengthening the training programme by working out the difficulties faced by learners and trainers; it is intended as a developmental intervention.

- *Awareness raising:* It leads to a process of collective awareness-raising. All the learners and the trainers are aware of what is happening to them at a given moment of time.
- *Empowering:* Because information is shared with the group, and the learners maintain control over the process of evaluation and its outcome, it becomes an empowering experience.
- *Mobilisation:* Learners are motivated towards contributing to the effectiveness of the training programme through such an evaluation process.

At the end of every day or each theme, ask the group to carry out a review of the relevance, content covered and the teaching method of the resource persons of the sessions covered.

At the end of the training programme, a written as well as an oral review may be carried out by the participants of the following aspects of the programme:

- Review of the Objectives and their Fulfilment:
  —Were the objectives realistic, simple and relevant?
  —Have they been achieved?
  —If so, to what extent?
  —What expectations remain unmet?
- Review of the Content and the Schedule
- Review of the Methods and Activities Used
- Review of the Trainers
- Review of the Scope of Participation
- Review of the Level of Discussion
- Review of the Group Process

- Review of the Reading Material
- Review of the Physical Environment

Organisational Plan

The organisational plan may include planning of the venue, equipment and budget.

Venue

The venue should be spacious enough for a circular or semi-circular arrangement of chairs, so that everyone can see each other and have adequate space for small group work in the centre.

Equipment

The equipment to be arranged by the organiser includes a black/white board and chalks; a flannel board and pins; chart papers, flip chart board and sketch pens, cello tape and scissors; overhead projector, transparencies and pens; and radio, audio cassette player, slide projector, video cassette player and television, if they are to be used. The participants should be asked to bring a diary and pen for themselves.

Use of Flannel Boards

One flannel board should be planned by the organisers to display the programme schedule, a relevant poem, quotations, fact sheets, news and so on. Another flannel board may be used for participants to express themselves in terms of satisfaction with the programme, output of the small group activities and so on.

Budget

The budget may include items such as rent for the venue, equipment, travel and transportation, lodging, board and honorarium for the resource persons, communication and stationery and photocopy charges. The participants' expenses such as their travel and transportation, lodging and board may either be budgeted, or they may be asked to pay for themselves, and/or they may be charged a fee to meet the expenses related to the organisation of the programme.

Note

This Chapter on Methodology of Progressive Training Programmes has its source in conducting Refresher Courses as well as the training programme I organised on Life Enrichment Programme and preparation of Sourcebooks for the same.

Chapter 6

Methodology of Progressive Social Work Knowledge Development

INTRODUCTION

According to Kearl (2004), "data" is defined as input gathered through the senses; and "information" as integrated data, which denotes a significant change in the environment. Information is converted to "knowledge" by interconnecting it with known concepts and skills as part of achieving a goal. "Wisdom" is knowledge about knowledge. Knowledge facilitates predicting, adapting to, and controlling both physical and social phenomena and change. Application of knowledge yields expertise, and additional analytical or experiential insights are said to constitute instances of wisdom (Britannica, 2001).

Knowledge, as an individual, organisational and societal resource, is stronger today than at any other time in history. However, knowledge does not exist objectively. The meaning, validity and use of knowledge depend upon the ideological perspective for development of the knowledge. Knowledge reflects the dominant ideology in the society and has the power to contribute to social transformation. It is, therefore, a major social responsibility to ensure socially transformative knowledge development and dissemination. Such knowledge development is particularly important for a profession with social responsibility at its core, such as the social work profession.

Institutions for social work education have a major role to play in development of social work knowledge. Social work educators are regularly in touch with the field as fieldwork instructors and also through their field action projects. However, the research methodologies useful for social work practice do not seem to have taken off in India. Social work educators, in most of the institutions for social work education, do not carry out research, for several reasons, such as research not being considered part of their workload, priority given to contribution to development of the field of practice, lack of infrastructural support and so on. Those who do carry out research seem to be more involved with research of the social phenomena that they are teaching and/or working with in the field. Citation and referencing are generally not given importance. As a result, researchers often do not disseminate their findings out of fear of plagiarism. The books that they do publish are generally on the social phenomena rather than on methods and skills of practice.

Social work practitioners generally do not document their practice or undertake research, and if they do, they tend to carry out *ad hoc* studies, without linking these to the existing state of knowledge. Since they do not publish their findings, these do not become retrievable and are not utilised by other social work professionals. They thus do not add to the body of social work knowledge.

This chapter starts with the concept and need for social work knowledge. It then examines the influence of progressive ideologies on social work knowledge development and the methodological developments and types of progressive social work research. It concludes with the steps and ethics for such social work research.

CONCEPT AND NEED FOR SOCIAL WORK KNOWLEDGE

Concept of Social Work Knowledge

Mattaini (1995) made a case that professionals and non-professionals may share similar values, it is knowledge that is the most distinctive aspect of professional practice. Since 1915, when Abraham Flexner concluded that social work was not a profession because it does not have a knowledge base, pursuit for professionalism has led social workers to work hard for a scientific knowledge base as well as specialised skills, techniques and functions. In fact, leadership of caseworkers in knowledge development on specialised skills is one of the main reasons that led to their subsequent dominance in the profession (Hopps and Pinderhughes, 1987). The question to be addressed is what is social work knowledge.

In the *Encyclopaedia of Social Work in India*, Herlekar (1968) used the term "social work literature" to include such literature which is related to or useful to social work. She grouped social work knowledge into three areas. The first is knowledge provided by social sciences, an area which is concerned with the knowledge of human beings in society, of human growth and behaviour and social problems. The second is knowledge of fields and programmes of social work, concerned with the organisation, administration and operation of social welfare programmes. The third is knowledge of social work practice, concerning the methods, processes and professional skills.

In the American *Encyclopedia of Social Work*, Khinduka (1987: 686) defined the knowledge base of social work more specifically as follows:

> The knowledge base of social work is a composite of knowledge produced indigenously by social workers themselves and, predominantly, of that derived from other disciplines By analysing and evaluating their own practice experiences and by selectively borrowing and adapting concepts from cognate disciplines and profession, social workers have developed various approaches [of intervention].

In my opinion, when the various social sciences study social phenomena/issues/problems in their varied dimensions, it is imperative for a profession such as social work to "base" its intervention on social science knowledge, and not just use it at the level of 'borrowing'. However, if social work intervention is based on social science knowledge, the base knowledge cannot be conceptualised as comprising social work knowledge. On the other hand, if all knowledge produced by social workers is to be included into social work knowledge, the substantive definition of what comprises social work knowledge becomes less important. Another conceptual mistake that takes place, in the Indian context, is to assume that all that is published in the journals of social work is social work literature. A study of articles published in *The Indian Journal of Social Work* (*IJSW*) by Vijayalakshmi, Devi Prasad and Rao (1996) revealed that social work professionals (educators/ practitioners) wrote less than a third of the articles published in the *IJSW* from 1970 to 1990.

Social work knowledge may be conceptualised as knowledge specific to the social work profession. It then covers various aspects of social work profession such as its origin and a history of development; its paradigms, values, goals and ethics; methods, practice and process of intervention; case records; research and knowledge building; education and training; curriculum plans; field instruction; specialisations; educators and students; employment and human power; professional associations; and so on. Thus defined, it may include literature developed by an author outside of the profession. On the other hand, literature developed on any social phenomenon by a social work professional, which does not draw any link with the profession, may not be considered social work literature.

According to Mattaini (1995), practice wisdom is knowledge passed on from generation to generation of social workers, sometimes as a form of oral tradition. Experienced social workers often have learned a tremendous amount that can be of value to others. He identifies two types of practice wisdom: (1) explicit rules that are handed down by experienced practitioners to others that appear to work; and (2) patterns of professional behaviour which may or may not be articulated, that have been shaped and refined over years of practice and serve as models for other workers. Social workers also base their work on their own life experiences, personal and professional.

Mattaini (1995) cautions that there are risks associated with a reliance on such rules. For example, accepted rules sometimes grow more from what works for the practitioner than what works for the client. It is, therefore, important for the social worker to constantly monitor whether approaches rooted in this body of knowledge contribute to meeting the clients' goals.

Need for Types of Social Work Knowledge

Social work profession needs different types of knowledge for its different functions, of practice, policy planning and administration, research and education and training. Social work practitioners need transformative knowledge to understand exclusion and the knowledge domain of people they work with and knowledge needed for their inclusion. They need to update themselves with developments in the field that impinge upon their practice; social work educators need to know the latest knowledge developed in order to update their curriculum and the recommended reading, students need to know what to read for their assignments and prepare for the examination and social work researchers need to comprehensively know the state of art of research in the field. Thus, the needs for different types of social work knowledge are as follows:

- Information on social work, welfare and development;
- Social work research;
- Organised social work knowledge for practice, policy planning and administration, education and training and research; and
- Bibliographic resources on social science, development studies and social work literature.

Information on Social Work, Welfare and Development

The following may be the main types of information on social work, welfare and development that the social work professionals need to have access to:

- Directories of voluntary organisations, professional associations, international organisations and academic institutions.
- Policies, schemes and reports of relevant ministries, departments and commissions of the central and state governments.
- Indian Constitution, social legislation and human rights instruments.
- Newsletters of social work professional associations for updates and reviews of social work education and practice.
- Newsletters and bulletins for updates and reviews of voluntary work and government laws, policies and schemes and so on.

Organised Social Work Knowledge

Any literature can be considered knowledge only when it is cumulatively organised to link new literature to previous ones and to theories. This linkage could be in the form of application, adaptation, elaboration or critique. Social work profession has to base its work on the understanding of social phenomena as studied by various social sciences. Reality needs to be understood holistically in order to plan intervention. Multidisciplinary literature developed as applied social science on issues and problems is more directly useful for social work.

Social work educators need knowledge necessary for teaching and training. Such knowledge can be organised in the forms of curriculum development, course compendia, teaching-learning resources, standards for social work education and so on. Encyclopaedia and dictionaries are reference books, concisely prepared out of a range of primary literature, most useful for any discipline or profession. Organising social work knowledge is also essential for development of a cumulative body of knowledge. Citations and referencing are, therefore, indispensable tasks in this process.

Bibliographic Resources on Social Science and Social Work Literature

The purpose of secondary literature is to "filter" the primary information sources, usually by subject area, and provide the indicators to this literature in the form of reviews, abstracts, annotations and indexes. These act as a gateway to several attributes of primary literature: authors, subjects, publishers, dates (and languages) of publication, and citations (Britannica, 2001). Social work educators and researchers need bibliographic resources on social sciences and social work literature.

PROGRESSIVE IDEOLOGIES AND SOCIAL WORK KNOWLEDGE

Modern ideologies of the western white world have considered science as the exemplar for discovering "truth", and "truth" (often described as reality) is equated only with the observable and measurable. Scientism rejects every method of inquiry other than scientific (Geiger, 1947). This ideology is challenged by emerging ideologies such as post-modernism, critical pedagogy and qualitative research.

The emerging ideology of post-modernism rejects attempts to apply the model of natural science inquiry in the social sciences (Rosenau, 1992) and critiques totality, reason and universality (Nicholson, 1990). Post-modernists recognise the highest ideals of modernity in the West as immanent to a specific historical time and geographical region and also associated with certain political baggage. Such a baggage includes notions of the supremacy of the West (Nicholson, 1990). In social work, high value has generally been attached to the American social work education model and American social work literature, which has now begun to be questioned. The American social work literature travels round the world fast, following the adoption of the American model for social work curriculum by different countries. Although there is value in learning from other countries, there are problems inherent in adopting knowledge developed in one country for use in social work practice in another country (Desai, 1997).

The ideology of post-modernism has brought about visibility to important ideological and structural forces, such as race, gender and class by acknowledging the question of power and value in the construction of knowledge and subjectivities. It has raised questions regarding how culture is inscribed in the production of centre/margin hierarchies and the reproduction of post-colonial forms of subjugation (Giroux, 1991). In modern society, knowledge, which sees truth as based in science, has been increasingly concentrated in the hands of "experts" and the elite class they represent. The claim to truth gives rise to hierarchies of knowledge, which reinforce and legitimate the economic and social hierarchies. As Foucault put it, the truth-claim and the procedures for gaining access to that truth have historically privileged the pronouncements of trained experts over the discourses of "ordinary" people. Underlying these elements of the power of expertise is the expert's lack of any accountability to the ordinary people affected by his or her knowledge (Sohng, 1995).

The political nature of knowledge is well illustrated by the fact that each of these privileged truths is being challenged – not primarily by alternative theories from the sciences but by the socio-political movements that Foucault called the "insurrection of subjugated knowledge". It provides forms of historical knowledge as a way of reclaiming power and identity for subordinate groups (Hartman, 1992). Transformative knowledge represents quests for knowledge that take account of perspectives, experiences and wisdom of the marginalised groups and excavate historically subjugated knowledge. In order to organise transformative knowledge, there is a need to critically identify the ideological base of the literature, examine the process of exclusion and assure inclusion of the marginalised groups (www.classes.csumb.edu/MAE/MAE637-01/world/elements/Transformative.html).

The post-modern understanding of knowledge-power linkage has brought about a painful paradox for social work professionals. As professionals, social workers possess knowledge and are experts because of their knowledge, but the power in their knowledge can disempower our clients. As Hartman (1992) suggested, they need to be open to local knowledge and participate with them in the insurrection of subjugated knowledge.

From a socially critical perspective, knowledge is constructed within our historical and cultural frameworks. Knowledge, according to the critical theorists, is historically, socially, economically and politically conditioned (Toohey, 1999). According to Giroux (1999), critical pedagogy attempts to do the following:

- Create new forms of knowledge through its emphasis on breaking down disciplines and creating interdisciplinary knowledge.

- Raise questions about the relationships between the margins and centres of power in schools and is concerned about how to provide a way of reading history as part of a larger project of reclaiming power and identity, particularly as these are shaped around the categories of race, gender, class and ethnicity.
- Reject the distinction between high and popular culture so as to make curriculum knowledge responsive to the everyday knowledge that constitutes people's lived histories differently.
- Illuminate the primacy of the ethical in defining the language that teachers and others use to produce particular cultural practices.

The post-modern reaction to modern ethical theories recommends that moral thinkers should turn their attention away from the problematic to the person as a whole. People's goodness has to do, not with virtues, but with their integrated wholeness (Agarwal, 1998). The paradigm of qualitative research relies on such holistic analysis and detailed description derived from close contacts with the participants of the study. The qualitative methodology tends to focus on techniques such as participant observation, semi-structured interviews and hermeneutic analysis of texts. Moreover, techniques such as presenting extensive direct quotations so readers can make their own judgements and having several other researchers examine the raw data to ensure that the findings do not reflect a single researcher's biases are critical (Mattaini, 1995). The qualitative approach is more suitable to social work as both have similar holistic and participatory philosophy. This approach is useful to synthesise social theory, practice and research (Ruckdeschel, 1985).

METHODOLOGICAL DEVELOPMENTS IN SOCIAL WORK RESEARCH

Traditionally, the ideal in social work research has been empiricism. However, as Austin (1979) stated, the legitimating of social work profession has depended on social utility rather than on its scientific base. He concluded that social work is a profession based on organised practitioner wisdom and is not, and probably will not be, a truly science-based profession in the foreseeable future. Goldstein (1990) noted that by adopting the scientific emphasis, intuition and commonsense ways of understanding were discredited. Emphasising the rigour of detached objectivity, scientism held little regard for subjective constructs such as morality, spirituality, and cultural or personal belief systems. Not the least, he says, a positivistic pre-occupation with instrumental means tended to overlook the profession's commitment to certain social ends. Goldstein concluded that social work practice has to be an ever-changing and complex blend of theory, analogue, wisdom and art.

As education of social work research has traditionally been modelled on pure social research, students of the professional course are trained for research, which can tell one the state of things as they are, than research that aims at bettering them. Social work students, therefore, fail to see a direct link between research and practice. As a result of such training, most of the social workers think that they have nothing to do with research. Such training makes social workers poor researchers and poor users of research in the practice situation. This explains why practitioners generally do not document their own work and analyse it. As a result, much of the contributions of social work practitioners to theory building remain irretrievable for the purpose of social work education.

Thomas (1979) observed that at best, social workers view the culmination of research as the drawing of conclusions from research findings that may have implications for social work, or be worthy of utilisation research, rather than as the generation of interventional or other social innovations that direct applications in the social technology of social work. He further noted that social work has been slow to recognise that its social technology is subject to systematic rather than incidental and haphazard alternation and that social work researchers and others in social work can participate actively in its generation.

Powers and others (1985) highlighted the need for a practitioner to make informed decisions. These decisions and subsequent practice behaviours are precisely the types of things that professionals should justify. They said that the ultimate test of effective knowledge building in any profession is the degree to which the body of knowledge is prescriptive. Social work profession thus requires knowledge-as-action. Such knowledge could be organised by linking social work practice wisdom with social science/work research/theories or drawing implications of social science/work research and theories for practice, towards development of praxis. Knowledge for practice, policy planning and administration may be organised in the forms of handbooks, manuals, standards for practice and so on.

Social intervention research, systematic review methods, research syntheses and meta-analysis, evidence-based practice and action and participatory research are important methodological developments in contemporary social work research that guides social work practice.

Social Intervention Research

Evaluation research gained increased importance in social work, in the 1970's, as a tool to ascertain accountability of social work organisations and programmes. Subsequently, single system design and developmental research, both of which contain the element of evaluation, developed as methodologies in social work research. Single system design facilitates a formative type of evaluation of practice with a system – be it an individual, family, group, organisation, community or other collectivity. The heart of single system design is collecting repeated information on the target problem alike time series research (Bloom and Fischer, 1982). Thomas (1979) developed the paradigm of developmental research, which is a combination of the models of research and development and research utilisation. Analysis, development and evaluation comprise the phases of research utilisation. As translated to social work research, this R & D approach became known as social intervention research. As a research-development methodology, social intervention research has provided the profession with a systematic, cumulative research methodology for developing, refining, testing and disseminating research-based social interventions. Accordingly, rather than wasting research resources on the evaluation of poorly conceptualised interventions, this methodology has contributed to the development and identification of interventions of proven effectiveness (Mullen, 2002).

In the early years of evaluation research, there were many flawed attempts to identify and measure social intervention outcomes. However, with experience and increased methodological prowess, the science of outcomes measurement has developed into a sophisticated specialisation (Mullen, 2002).

Systematic Review Methods, Research Syntheses and Meta-Analysis

While the outcome of a single evaluation may be cause for attention, one study does not establish a foundation for decision-making. In the early 1970's social work researchers used narrative reviews to summarise findings from groups of evaluations, sometimes using systematic methods and sometimes not. When few studies existed, this approach served the profession well. As studies increased, without explicit, systematic review methods such overviews were subject to unknown bias. Accordingly, the development of systematic review methods as well as sophisticated, quantitative meta-analytic procedures has made it possible to specify with greater confidence and precision the combined outcomes of many studies. The growth of methodological sophistication in the review and syntheses of outcomes from multiple studies has been a singularly important methodological development in the move towards evidence-based approaches (Mullen, 2002).

Evidence-based Practice

Evidence-based practice (EBP) is an emerging approach in the United Kingdom, which means any practice that has been established as effective through scientific research according to some set of explicit criteria (Mullen, 2002). According to Gambrill (2003), EBP suggests a philosophy of practice and policy designed to honour ethical obligations to clients and students and an evolving technology for helping us to do so. Professionals have an obligation to inform clients about services found to be effective and to avoid harm. Concerns that practitioners were continuing to use methods found to be harmful was a key reason for the development of EBP. EBP encourages transparency of what is done to what effect in all venues of interest including practice and policy, research and professional education. It is designed to make decisions and the reasons for them explicit. EBP involves sharing responsibility for decision-making in a context of recognised uncertainty. It is this characteristic of transparency that is such a break with authority-based practice and policy, research and professional education (Gambrill, 2003).

Gambrill (2003) further states that EBP describes a process designed to encourage integration of ethical, evidentiary and application concerns. It involves a systemic approach to improving quality of services including the following:

- Efforts to educate professionals who are life-long learners,
- Involving clients as informed participants who take part in decisions made,
- Attending to management practices and policies that influence practice (that is, evidence-based purchase of services), and
- Attending to application challenges including the implications of scarce resources.

EBP and social care are designed to maximise flow of accurate information concerning the evidentiary status of practice-related claims including information about harming in the name of helping.

Action and Participatory Research

O'Brien (1998) defined action research as aiming to contribute both to the practical concerns of people in an immediate problematic situation and to further the goals of social science simultaneously. Thus, there is a dual commitment in action research to study a system and concurrently to collaborate with members of the system in changing it in what is together regarded as a desirable direction. Accomplishing this twin goal requires the active collaboration of researcher and client, and thus it stresses the importance of co-learning as a primary aspect of the research process. Several attributes separate action research from other types of research. Primary is its focus on turning the people involved into researchers, too – people learn best, and more willingly apply what they have learned, when they do it themselves. It also has a social dimension – the research takes place in real-world situations, and aims to solve real problems. Finally, the initiating researcher, unlike in other disciplines, makes no attempt to remain objective, but openly acknowledges their bias to the other participants (O'Brien, 1998).

Following are the six principles of action research identified by Winter (1989, cited from O'Brien, 1998):

- *Reflective critique:* The principle of reflective critique ensures people that reflect on issues and processes and makes explicit the interpretations, biases, assumptions and concerns upon which judgements are made. In this way, practical accounts can give rise to theoretical considerations.
- *Dialectical critique:* Reality, particularly social reality, is consensually validated, which is to say it is shared through language. Phenomena are conceptualised in dialogue.
- *Collaborative resource:* Participants in an action research project are co-researchers. The principle of collaborative resource pre-supposes that each person's ideas are equally significant as potential resources for creating interpretive categories of analysis, negotiated among the participants.

- *Risk:* The change process potentially threatens all previously established ways of doing things, thus creating psychic fears among the practitioners.
- *Plural structure:* The nature of the research embodies a multiplicity of views, commentaries and critiques, leading to multiple possible actions and interpretations. This plural structure of inquiry requires a plural text for reporting.
- *Theory, practice and transformation:* For action researchers, theory informs practice, practice refines theory, in a continuous transformation. In any setting, people's actions are based on implicitly held assumptions, theories and hypotheses, and with every observed result, theoretical knowledge is enhanced.

Originally designed to resist the intellectual colonialism of western social research into the Third World development process, participatory research developed a methodology for involving disenfranchised people as researchers in pursuit of answers to the questions of their daily struggle and survival. Based in Paulo Freire's ideology, participatory research is a means of putting research capabilities in the hands of deprived and disenfranchised people so that they can identify themselves as knowing actors; defining their reality, shaping their new identity, naming their history, and transforming their lives for themselves (Sohng, 1995).

Finn (1994, cited from Sohng, 1995) outlined three key elements, namely, people, power and praxis, which distinguish participatory research from traditional approaches to social science:

- Participatory research is people-centred in the sense that the process of critical inquiry is informed by and responds to the experiences and needs of oppressed people.

- Participatory research is about power, which is crucial to the construction of reality, language, meanings and rituals of truth. Participatory research promotes empowerment through the development of common knowledge and critical awareness, which are suppressed by the dominant knowledge system.
- Participatory research is also about praxis. It recognises the inseparability of theory and practice and critical awareness of the personal-political dialectic.

Participatory research is grounded in an explicit political stance and clearly articulated value base – social justice and the transformation of those contemporary socio-cultural structures and processes that support degeneration of participatory democracy, injustice and inequality.

TYPES OF SOCIAL WORK RESEARCH ACCORDING TO STAGES OF PRACTICE

Desai (1992) classified social work research according to the purpose it serves depending upon the stage of practice in which it is conducted, as discussed below:

Research in the Planning Stage of Practice

Research in the planning stage of practice may be carried out in order to plan or ascertain appropriateness of the plan for practice (Epstein and Tripodi, 1979).

Need Analysis: While studying the plan of practice, it is essential to ascertain that it is based on the actual and felt needs of the potential beneficiaries, depending upon their situation. Such baseline data may be obtained through need analysis. Some objective criteria, to establish the need conditions for the specific intervention, will first have to be theoretically worked out, based on the expected outcome. All the individuals in an age group may need developmental intervention, whereas specific outcome may have to be laid down for need for remedial intervention. According to Carter (1960), the need conditions may be those expressed by clients and those unexpressed by clients. For the needs expressed by the clients, they may or may not be utilising the services.

Survey of Similar Programmes: At the stage of initiating a programme, it is also important to carry out a survey of similar programmes that may exist in the city. Gaps in these services indicate the need for extension of new services. If similar programmes are available, the need survey may also examine whether the potential beneficiaries are using these services. If they are not, the reasons may be examined.

A need analysis may be used in three major ways:

1. The scope of the programme may be planned according to the magnitude of people concluded as needing the intervention.
2. The characteristics of the people needing the intervention can be useful while planning the content of the intervention.
3. The difficulties people report in utilising services of similar programmes are useful for planning the service delivery aspects of practice.

Resource Survey: At the stage of planning of practice, a resource survey may also be carried out in the defined locality in order to compile information needed for providing information and referral services to the beneficiaries. Such a survey may explore number and types of services available, and provided by organisations as well as individuals to meet a particular need. Criteria for intake of clientele for these services are also important to examine in such a survey.

Research in the Implementation Stage of Practice

According to Morris and Fitz-Gibbon (1978), formative evaluation of programme implementation is known as programme monitoring and summative evaluation of the same is known as programme documentation. They further specify that monitoring often means assuming a role in the programme planning, development and refinement. It helps the staff and the planners to identify obstacles, implement changes and make additions to the programmes as it develops. Morris and Fitz-Gibbon describe programme documentation as useful for accountability, providing a lasting description of the programme and a list of the possible causes of the programme's effects.

Monitoring and documentation at the implementation stage may be carried out of the following:

1. Check the implementation of intervention with reference to the goals set and the plan formulated,
2. Examine its utilisation by the designated population and satisfaction of the beneficiaries,
3. Analyse the problem,
4. Ascertain the process of change and the intermediate outcome of the intervention, and
5. Review the relevant theories.

Different types of organisational studies and studies of service delivery systems may be carried out in order to assess the implementation of an intervention.

Through a service utilisation study, one can ascertain the extent to which the designated target population is being reached. Such a study may identify difficulties in service utilisation by people, such as lack of awareness, cultural or personal obstacles, long distance, transportation difficulties, service insufficient, strict intake criteria, and so on.

Opinion/attitude studies for the intervention may assess service utilisation as well as acceptance of the intervention. The targets for such studies may be the staff or the beneficiaries.

A periodic review of the case records of the agency is useful for several purposes:

1. It is another way to examine whether the programme reaches the designated target population.
2. It is useful to analyse the problems people come with.
3. It can show the trend in people's problem manifestations over a period of time.
4. The process of the practitioner's intervention can be examined through such a review.
5. The process of change and the intermediate outcome of the intervention can be analysed through such a review.

Such an analysis feeds into the documentation of the programme efforts that helps to study what led to the final outcome of the programme. A valuable outcome of such a review is that it also helps in arriving at an improved case recording system.

Research in the Conclusion Stage of Practice

Research in the conclusion stage of practice is same as summative evaluation with reference to effectiveness and efficiency. Such a study will be useful for making improvements in the intervention approach, reviewing the theories behind practice and repeating or replicating the practice.

Effectiveness of practice may be examined by comparing the outcome with the baseline data and the expected outcome.

Rosen and Proctor (1979) have classified outcome into three types:

1. Intermediate outcomes, which are presumed to contribute to or create a facilitative climate for continuation of the programme. Assessment of the intermediate outcome may be done at the implementation stage of the intervention.
2. Instrumental outcomes, which, when achieved, are assumed to lead necessarily to the achievement of the programme goals without the help of the programme.
3. Ultimate outcomes are indicators of achievement of the programme goals. The instrumental outcome may be assessed at the conclusion stage, whereas a follow-up study is needed to assess the ultimate outcome of practice.

Efficiency of practice may be assessed by a cost-benefit analysis of the outcome with reference to the resources or efforts put in.

ETHICS OF SOCIAL WORK RESEARCH

The Declaration of Ethics for Professional Social Workers by Bombay Association of Trained Social Workers (2002) lists the following ethical best practices for social work research:

Professional social workers:

- Carefully select the topic for research considering its possible consequences for those studied, when conducting a research.
- Do not cause the respondents any physical or mental discomfort, distress or harm, through research.
- Consider the informants of research as co-partners in understanding the phenomenon.

- Share their research objectives with them and get their informed and voluntary consent, respect their knowledge and attitude about their life situation, and share/interpret the findings with them.
- Protect the confidentiality of the information shared by them and use the findings for their benefit, by recommending and promoting policies and programmes concerning them.
- Provide information and referral services to them, as and when necessary, during the process of data collection.
- Dissociate from or do not engage in any research activity, which requires manipulation, distortion or falsification of data or findings.

Note

This Chapter on Methodology of Progressive Social Work Knowledge Development has its source in my work with a research unit in the Institute, the Unit for Family Studies, which was then linked to the social work Department of Family and Child Welfare. Besides carrying out social work research and publishing articles on it, I conducted workshops with students on how social work research has to apply social research methodology to improve social work practice. I also published a Special Issue of *The Indian Journal of Social Work* (*IJSW*) on 'Social Work Literature'.

CHAPTER 7

Methodology of Progressive Social Work Knowledge Dissemination and Retrieval

INTRODUCTION

Knowledge is developed for utilisation and utilisation needs a system of dissemination and retrieval. For dissemination of social work knowledge, it is important to understand the methodology of publication. Retrieval of social work knowledge is mainly through libraries and Internet. This chapter discusses these aspects.

METHODOLOGY OF PUBLICATION

Publication is the major system for dissemination of any knowledge, because of its quality control system of style and review, copy editing and proofreading, production and marketing network. As published literature is easy to acquire by libraries, it is easy to utilise it and thus makes further development of knowledge possible.

Editorial Board, Editor and Editorial Style

For social work publications, the editorial board and the editor should be drawn mainly from social work educators, who would be familiar with the state of the art, criteria and process for review and further need for social work knowledge. The editorial board adopts a standardised editorial style or develops one. An editorial style includes norms for organisation of the typescript (TS), language, presentation style and the reference style. The importance of professional journals comes from their use of recognised norms judged by other experts, using pre-established impersonal criteria in an open intellectual arena (Kirk, 1999).

The editorial boards also need to lay down ethical guidelines for authorship, referencing, acknowledgements, using and promoting stereotypes, protecting confidentiality, accuracy of facts and so on.

Review System

The criteria used for judging the suitability of the TS for publication are generally the following: contemporary relevance, contribution to knowledge, conceptual clarity and logic in analysis, readable language, sound methodology of research articles, implications for intervention, appropriateness of references and originality.

In the review process, the TS is processed either by the editor or by one/two referees through a two-way masked peer review. The reviewers or the referees would use the above criteria and conclude whether the TS is acceptable for publication, needs revision or is rejected. When the reports of the two referees do not match, the TS is either sent to a third referee or the editor reviews it. If the review suggests revision of the TS, the author(s) are given time for revision and re-submission. The revised and re-submitted TS is then sent to the same referee(s) for checking the revisions. Invited typescripts are not sent for a review.

Editing

A book editor or a guest editor for a special issue of a journal generally plays the following role:

- Identifies a theme.
- Invites abstracts of articles from prospective authors and sends the guidelines to be followed by the selected authors.
- Reviews the articles received, that is, accept, send for revisions or reject the articles.
- Edits the accepted articles for subject matter and for the publisher's editorial style.
- Obtains the missing information and clarifies contradictions with the authors.
- Ensures that written permissions are obtained from copyright owners whenever necessary.
- Check the page proofs.

Copy Editing

After a TS has been accepted for publication, it needs copy editing for grammar, language, presentation style, organisation and flow, and references, before it is sent for typesetting. This is necessary for making it readable and free of errors.

The author is, of course, an expert on the subject of the TS, but another keen eye can pick up errors and inconsistencies generally not detected by the author. The author's focus is normally on the content and exposition of the subject. Matters of language, presentation and organisation might take the back seat – some authors do not know these, some just do not care, and many do not want to "get distracted" by attention to language, while focusing on the presentation of thought. Moreover, the authors may get jaded in expression and go through a million moods before they complete the writing. They get blind and may miss out what another reader readily identifies as incorrect or inconsistent or illogical. The copy editors have a trained eye – an eye trained for the purpose of identifying these "slips".

Proof-reading

After the copy-edited matter is typeset, it can be printed as proofs. Proof-reading is the process of checking and correcting the proofs, word for word, against the original copy-edited TS, or the latest proof against the previous proof.

Proof-reading is an immensely important aspect of the publishing process, but tends to be underrated. Proof-reading helps to determine the ultimate credibility of a document in that, if it is printed with spelling mistakes and editorial and design/layout inconsistencies, its authority will, to a large extent, be undermined.

Production

Since the 1960's volume publishing has become an automated process using large computers and high-speed printers to transfer digitally stored data on paper. The appearance of microcomputer-based publishing system has proved to be another significant advance. Economical enough to allow even small organisations to become in-house publishers, this so-called desktop publishing system is able to format text and graphics interactively on a high-resolution video screen with the aid of page-description command languages. Once a page has been formatted, the entire image is transferred to an electronic printing or photo-composition device (Britannica, 2001).

Types of Social Work Publications

Social work knowledge may be published in the following ways:

- *Articles:* Writing an article in a newspaper/newsletter/ magazine, journal or an edited book.
- *Books:* Writing or editing a book.
- *Periodicals:* Editing a newsletter, a journal, special issues of a journal, a series or an encyclopaedia.

Journals

Journals play a fundamental role in the development of all disciplines and professions. They create a record of how well professions meet one of the requirements of professions: possession of a body of knowledge. Journals serve to preserve and document the past, disseminate information from contemporary scholars, and aid the development of the profession's knowledge base by identifying appropriate contributions and preserving them in an archival source (Lindsey and Kirk, 1992).

Social work journals can cover the following types of literature:

- Theoretical/historical/empirical/methodological/ epistemological analyses

- Reviews of policies/programmes/legislation/voluntary organisations/professional interventions
- Curriculum development/teaching aids
- Research summaries
- News from professional associations in social work
- Book reviews and media reviews
- Discussions, notes and interviews

Writing for Publication

The methodology of writing the TS is important for organising knowledge that can be worthy of publication. It comprises of organisation of the TS, language, presentation style and reference style, as discussed below. Consistency should be maintained at in all these aspects from the opening to the concluding statement.

Organisation of the Typescript

Components: Besides the title and the text, a typescript, sometimes also includes the following:

- Foreword/Preface/Acknowledgements
- Tables and figures
- Notes
- References

Title: The following aspects need to be considered while formulating the title of the TS.

- The title should normally not exceed beyond 12 words.
- It should be appropriate for the content, summarise the main idea of the TS and be fully explanatory when standing alone. Words that serve no purpose should be

avoided. For example, in the title 'Report of a Study of an Investigation into the Deaths of Tribal Children in Balaghat District of Madhya Pradesh', the first nine words are redundant.

- Some manuscripts may have a sub-title. The sub-title follows the title with a colon separating them. Two sub-titles should be avoided.

Text: The text includes the introduction, conclusion and the sections in between the two: The first section of the book should introduce the topic, the theme and the objectives and define the key concepts discussed. It should not be too long. This section may or may not carry the title "Introduction".

The last section should wrap up the article by re-stating the theme in a concluding manner and draw implications for policies, programmes, implications and further research. It should not present new data.

Between the "Introduction" and the "Conclusion", the book should be divided into major sections, according to the major components of the theme. A long section should be divided into relevant sub-sections. There should be appropriate transitions between sections.

Headings indicate the organisation of the manuscript in terms of major sections, sub-sections within sections and so on. All topics of equal importance have the same order/level of headings throughout a TS. Different levels of headings may be presented as follows:

LEVEL 1: BOLD AND UPPERCASE (for main sections).

Level 2: Bold and Title Case (for sub-sections within the main sections).

Level 3: Bold, Title Case and Italicised (for sub-sub-sections within the sub-sections).

Level 4: Bold and Title Case: The text continue after a colon.

Level 5: Not Bold, Title Case and Italicised (for sub-sub-sub sections within the sub-sub-sections).

Style for Analysis of a Topic: The following aspects of style are useful for analysis of a topic:

- Each statement may be supported by citation of another author's work, logical explanation, illustrations or the author's opinions.
- Notes from one library source may fit into more than one section of the paper. Sort out the notes accordingly.
- Notes from different sources relevant to one section may be organised into a coherent narration. If they pertain to one idea, they may be presented chronologically. The section may be concluded by observing the trends or the similarities and dissimilarities of different data.
- The first time a research is cited, give some information about the objectives, sample and the place of the study.
- Footnotes may be used to supplement or amplify substantive information in the text.

Paragraphs: Paragraphs may be planned as follows:

- Each paragraph should be developed around a main idea.
- One-sentence paragraphs are abrupt and should be avoided. On the other hand, too long a paragraph loses the reader's attention, and should, therefore, be broken up at appropriate places.

- Sentences making up a paragraph should relate to one another and hang together as a cohesive unit.
- There should be appropriate transitions between paragraphs, indicating elaboration, contradiction, comparison, conclusion and so on.

Tables and Figures: A horizontal table should be placed with the title on the left hand side. While it is necessary to draw attention to the highlights of the table in the text, mere repetition should be avoided. A figure may be a chart, graph, photograph, drawing or any other depiction.

Tables and figures should be numbered separately, followed by their respective titles of the table.

If the author has presented a table or figure in totality from a published work, permission to reproduce them from the respective copyright holder is necessary. Any qualifying information should be mentioned in a note below the table or the figure, before mentioning the source.

Notes: Notes for the text are explanatory statements that develop an idea or expand a quotation, where to do so in the text would disturb the flow. Notes may be placed as footnotes or endnotes, at the end of the text, before the acknowledgement and the references. Begin numbering notes from 1 for every article. The numbering should be indicated in the text by superscript figures outside the punctuation.

Acknowledgements: In case of an article, acknowledgement is placed at the end of the text matter, after the notes and before the references. However, in books, it comes in the beginning before the main text starts.

Language

Besides grammar, the syntax, economy of expression, parochialism and non-discriminatory language are important aspects in the TS.

Syntax: Syntax covers the following aspects:

- Sentence fragments, without minimally a subject and a verb, need to be avoided. For example, "How about that!" is a sentence fragment.
- Run-on sentences need to be separated or properly connected.
- Past tense is appropriate to cite other authors and to describe the results of a study. Present tense is appropriate for discussion and conclusions.
- Active voice should be preferred to passive voice.
- Pronouns 'I' or 'We' should be used for the author(s).
- Non-human sources should not be attributed human functions. For example, instead of "aspirations of social work", use "aspirations of social work professionals".
- Prefer to use "Seven studies have been done" to "There were seven studies done".

Economy of Expression: Wordiness, redundancy, overgeneralisation, clichés, slang and colloquial expressions should be avoided:

- Examples of wordiness are: "What we wish to say is that", "A large, big, huge organisation".
- Examples of redundant words are 'final' outcome, 'free' gift, and so on. Such words need to be deleted.

- Over-generalising expressions such as 'always', 'never', 'all' and 'none' should be avoided. Prefer to use 'often', 'generally', 'rarely', 'most', 'hardly' and so on.

Clichés or colloquial expressions are wordy and worn out. Instead, appropriate and simple words should be used. For example:

Avoid	*Prefer*
all in all	altogether
as luck would have it	fortunately
give rise to	cause
go without saying	be obvious
holy state of matrimony	marriage
in hot soup	in trouble
put one's nose to the grindstone	work hard
wheel of fortune	fate

Parochialism: Parochialism needs to be avoided, as shown below:

- 'This country' should be replaced with the name of the country.
- 'Last year' and 'this year' should be replaced with the specific years.

Non-Discriminatory Language: Non-discriminatory language needs to be avoided as shown below:

- Constructions that might imply bias against or stereotypes on the basis of gender, ethnicity, disability or age should be avoided and replaced with non-discriminatory language.
- The use of 'male-specific' and 'male-identified' words in the generic sense should be avoided and replaced with terms such as humans, human race, human beings,

human species, humanity, humankind or women and men, person(s), man and woman, individual(s), people(s), and so on.

- Instead of using words that label people, their situation should be described. For example:

Avoid	*Prefer*
servant	domestic worker
aged	elderly/older person
delinquent	child in conflict with law
disabled	with disability
illegitimate	born out of wedlock
divorcee	person after divorce

- An ethnic group should not be trivialised by describing it with words such as 'culturally backward'.
- A family situation should not be denigraded with words such as 'broken family'.

Presentation

The presentation style includes spellings, punctuation, parentheses and brackets, capitalisation, numerals, italicisation and abbreviations. Words with hyphenation, italics, peculiar spellings, capitalisation and so on need to be consistent throughout.

Parentheses and Brackets: Parentheses ( ) are used to enclose additional material in a sentence and to enclose sources of a citation/reference. Brackets [ ] are used to enclose words within parentheses or quotations.

Capitalisation: Capitalise the first letters of proper nouns and proper adjectives. Use lower case for words like government, church, state, party, volume, and so on, unless part of a proper noun. If in doubt, and prefer capitalisation, use it all along, consistently.

Numerals:

1. The following numbers may be expressed in figures:
    - Numbers 10 and above.
    - Numbers that represent statistical functions.
    - Numbers that represent time, date, age, sample or population size, and exact sums of money.
    - Page numbers.
2. The following numbers may be expressed in words:
    - Numbers under 10.
    - Any number that begins a sentence, title or heading.
    - Common fractions, for example, third, three-fourths.
    - One of two adjacent numbers.
3. Dates may be presented as follows:
    - Dates should be set out as follows: July 8, 1980 or 8 July 1980.
    - Decades should be mentioned in figures, without an apostrophe; for example, 1980s.
    - Ordinality of dates should be expressed in words; for example, use nineteenth century instead of 19th century.
4. When 'from' precedes the first number, 'to' must precede the second number.
5. The percentage sign should be replaced with 'per cent'. For example, use 24 per cent instead of 24%.
6. Minimum numbers should not be used. For example, use 25–28, instead of 25–8.

Italicisation: The following are the norms for italicisation:

- All words foreign to English must be italicised and should be followed by its meaning in English in parentheses, when it is used for the first time.
- Caste names need to be capitalised and not italicised, as they are considered to be proper nouns.
- Names of plays, books and films should be italicised.
- Be sparing in italics for emphasis. The structure of a sentence and usage of words should, in itself, provide the necessary emphasis.

Abbreviations: The following are the norms for abbreviations:

- Foreign language abbreviations should be replaced with English words as follows:

Avoid	*Prefer*
etc.	and so on
viz.	namely
e.g.	for example
i.e.	that is
et al.	and others

- Text-specific abbreviations may be used, after spelling them out fully, giving the abbreviated letters in parentheses the first time they are used, for example, non-government organisations (NGOs). Even, the commonly known ones like the UN need to be spelt out the first time these are used.
- A sentence, title or section should not begin with an abbreviation.

- The use of apostrophes should be avoided as far as possible. For example, prefer, "the editor of the newspaper" to "the newspaper's editor".

Reference Style

The reference style includes the style for citation in the text, quotations and the reference list in the end of the TS, as discussed below:

Citation/Paraphrasing in the Text: Each statement, in the TS, may be supported by the author with a logical explanation, the author's opinion, illustration, or citation/ paraphrasing of another author's work. Without citing the source, use of others' written work amounts to plagiarism and, thereby, fraud.

Citation in the text briefly identifies the source for the readers, and enables them to locate the details of the source in the References at the end of the TS. Generally, the last name of the author and the year of publication, separated by a comma, are cited in the text. Following are some guidelines for citation in the text:

1. When the cited author has significantly contributed to the statement made, place his or her name in the narrative with the year of publication in the narrative or in parentheses. When the author is the source of information that could be obtained from several other sources, place his or her name and the year, separated by a comma, in parentheses, at the end of the statement.
2. When the references include publications by two or more authors with the same last name, include these author's initials in all text citations.

3. When a source has two authors, always cite both their names.
4. When a source has more than two authors, cite the names of all the authors the first time the citation is made. In the subsequent citations, include only the last name of the first author followed by 'and others'.
5. When the source of a citation is another citation, list the cited author and year of his/her publication, separated by a comma, state 'cited from' and then mention the author and year of the source. The references will, in this case, include only the latter source.
6. Order the citation of two or more sources, within the same parentheses, in the alphabetical order.
7. Within a paragraph, the year of the citation need not be repeated.
8. When a reference has no author, cite the first two to three words of the title and then ellipses (...), in place of the author's last name.

Quotations: Quotations are word-by-word reproduction from another author's work. A short quotation (fewer than 40 words) may be incorporated in the text, enclosed with single quotation marks. Please note that the punctuation (full stop, comma) falls inside the quotation mark if the material quoted is a complete sentence. Citation of the source of the quoted material should include page numbers.

Quoted material of over 40 words in length should be set out from the text by indenting five spaces from the left margin, with a line space above and below. Please note that indented quotations should not have quotation marks, unless they report conversation. For example:

> The distinction between movements and campaigns, for which there appears to be little precedent in the existing literature on movements, was made on the presupposition that there seem to be two distinct sets of phenomenon, though at times, the distinction may be one of degree, and they may slide into each other, or move from one into the other. For instance, campaigns may emerge from or link with movements or, at times, a campaign may take on a movement like dimension (Monteiro and Lingam, 1998: 3).

Ellipses are used in quotations to show that a word or words have been left out. Three dots indicate missing words at the beginning or within a sentence. Four dots show missing words at the end of the quote. Quoted material should not be edited.

Reproduction of a quotation of more than 500 words requires permission from the respective copyright holder.

References: The References, at the end of the TS, should provide complete information necessary to identify and retrieve each source cited in the article, text, tables or figures. The reference style generally includes the names of all the authors, year of publication, title of the article or the book, title of the journal or the edited book in which the article is published and publication details. The style with which these are sequenced varies from publisher to publisher.

Each entry in the references must be cited in the text. Both should be identical in spellings and year. Arrange entries in the References in the alphabetical order by the last name of the first author and then by his/her initials.

METHODOLOGY OF RETRIEVAL OF SOCIAL WORK KNOWLEDGE

Library science has been a profession for quite some time which is today well-equipped with Information Technology to facilitate retrieval of different types of knowledge. The libraries of institutions for social work education need to acquire and facilitate retrieval of the following:

1. Social work literature:
   - All the Indian social work literature, that is, encyclopaedias, books, journals, bibliographies, annotations and abstracts and newsletters and bulletins published in English and the local language.
   - All the social work encyclopaedias, dictionaries, annotations, abstracts and reviews published abroad.
   - All the publications of local, national and international social work professional associations.
   - All the international social work books and journals.
   - Select social work books and journals published abroad on basic social work subjects and fieldwork practicum.
   - Select books on foundation social sciences and optional/specialisation/concentration subjects of social work.
2. Government documents:
   - Census data
   - Five-Year Plans
   - Policies, schemes and reports of relevant ministries, departments and commissions of the central and the state governments.

- Publications of the United Nations (UN) and other international organisations working in India.

3. Books on Development Studies.
4. Directories of voluntary organisations and published and unpublished literature developed by these.
5. Newspapers and news magazines.
6. In-house documents:
   - Faculty research reports and publications
   - Student term papers/research reports/dissertations/theses

An annual index needs to be prepared of acquisition by the library. Inter-library exchange and linkages with the Information Library Network (INFLIBNET) should be facilitated. Literature can be made available on alternate media for visually disabled persons. Book banks can be facilitated. Archival and out-of-print reports and books need to be digitalised. An advisory committee needs to guide the functioning of the library.

The systems of social work knowledge dissemination and retrieval are going through changes in the world of information and knowledge increasingly being dominated by Internet. The explosive growth of communications networks after 1990, particularly in the scholarly world, has accelerated the establishment of the "virtual library". At the leading edge of this development is public-domain information. Residing in thousands of databases distributed worldwide, a growing portion of this vast resource is now accessible almost instantaneously via the Internet, the web of computer networks linking the global communities of researchers and, increasingly, non-academic organisations. Internet resources of electronic information include selected library catalogues, collected works of the literature, some abstracting journals, full-text electronic journals, encyclopaedias, software archives, demographic registers, daily news summaries, environmental reports, as well as hundreds of thousands of electronic-mail and bulletin-board messages (Britannica, 2001).

While the Internet has made the global information and knowledge easily accessible, it has thrown open a new challenge to the Indian social work professionals to learn to critically evaluate this knowledge, disseminate the Indian social work knowledge through this worldwide web, which is also dominated by the American literature, and develop a new system of professional conversation and enhancement of social work knowledge across the globe in the electronic mode.

Note

The Chapter on Methodology of Progressive Social Work Knowledge Dissemination and Retrieval emerged during my tenure as the Associate Editor of *IJSW*. My work in this position culminated in preparation of a Handbook of Management of *IJSW* and organising a National Workshop on Knowledge Development and Dissemination of Social Work Knowledge, on the 60th Anniversary of the journal. A Special Issue of *IJSW* on this theme is in press.

References

Agarwal, M.M., 1998, *Ethics and Spirituality*. Shimla: Indian Institute of Advanced Study.

Austin, D.N., 1979, Research and Social Work: Educational Paradoxes and Possibilities, *Journal of Social Service Research*, 2(2), 159-176.

Barker, R.L., 1987, *The Social Work Dictionary*. Silver Spring. Maryland: National Association of Social Workers.

Bloom, M. and Fischer, J., 1982, *Evaluation Practice: Guidelines for the Accountable Professional*. New Jersey: Prentice Hall, Inc.

Bombay Association of Trained Social Workers, 2002, Declaration of Ethics for Professional Social Workers. Mumbai.

Bombyk, M., 1995, Progressive Social Work. In *Encyclopedia of Social Work*. Washington, D.C.: National Association of Social Workers, 1933-1942.

Boyce, M., 1996, Teaching Critically as an Act of Praxis and Resistance (www.Newton.uor/FacultyFolder/Mboyce/1CRITPED.HTM).

Carter, G.W., 1966, Measurement of Need. In N.A. Polinsky (Ed.) *Social Work Research*. Chicago: The University of Chicago Press, 201-222.

Courneyer, D.E. and Klein, W.C., 2000, *Research Methods for Social Work*. Boston: Allyn and Bacon.

Desai, M. (Ed.), 1997, "Social Work Literature", Special Issue of *The Indian Journal of Social Work,* 58(2).

Dominelli, L., 2002, *Feminist Social Work Theory and Practice.* New York: Palgrave.

Epstein, I. and Tripodi, T., 1979, Incorporating Research into Macro Social Work Practice and Education. In A. Rubin and A. Rosenblatt (Eds.) *Sourcebook on Research Utilisation.* New York: Council for Social Work Education, 121-131.

Eraut, M., 1989, Selecting and Justifying Objectives. In M. Eraut (Ed.) *The International Encyclopaedia of Educational Methodology.* Oxford: Pergamon Press, 338-341.

Gambrill, E.D., 2003, Evidence-Based Practice: Sea Change or the Emperor's New Clothes?, *Journal of Social Work Education,* 39(1).

Gay, G., 1989, *Curriculum Development.* The International Encyclopaedia of Educational Methodology. Oxford: Pergamon Press, 467-476.

Geiger, G.R., 1947, *Philosophy and the Social Order: An Introductory Approach. Boston:* Houghton Mifflin Co.

Gibbs, L. and Gambrill, E., 1999, *Critical Thinking for Social Workers: Exercises for the Helping Profession.* Thousand Oaks, California: Pine Forge Press.

Giroux, H., 1999, What is Critical Pedagogy? (www.perfectfit.org/CT/giroux2.html).

Goldstein, H., 1990, The Knowledge Base of Social Work Practice: Theory, Analogue, or Art? *Families in Society: The Journal of Contemporary Human Services,*

Gough, J., 1997, *Developing Learning Materials.* Hyderabad: Orient Longman.

Hartman, A., 1992, In Search of Subjugated Knowledge, *Social Work,* 37(6).

Hartman, A. and Laird, J., 1983, *Family-Centred Social Work Practice.* New York: The Free Press.

Heany, T., 1995, Issues in Freirian Pedagogy. (www.nl.edu/ace/Resources/Documents/FreireIssues.html).

Herlekar, A., 1968, Literature of Social Work. In *Encyclopaedia of Social Work in India,* Volume 2, Delhi: Planning Commission.

Hokenstad, M.C. and Rigby, B.D., 1977, *Participation in Teaching and Learning: An Idea Book for Social Work Educators.* New York: International Association of Schools of Social Work.

Hopps, J.G. and Pinderhughes, E.B., 1987, Profession of Social Work: Contemporary Characteristics. In *Encyclopaedia of Social Work,* Silver Spring, Maryland: National Association of Social Workers, 351-366.

Institute of Cultural Affairs, 1991a, An Introduction to Discussion Method.

Institute of Cultural Affairs, 1991b, The Workshop Method.

IQRA, 2002, Course Guide (www.iqra-careers.com/c10.html).

Johnson, D.W., 1986, *Reaching Out: Interpersonal Effectiveness and Self-Actualisation*, New Jersey: Prentice-Hall.

Kearl, M.C., 2004, Sociology of Knowledge. Department of Sociology and Anthropology, University of Colorado at Denver. (www.trinity.edu/~mkearl/knowledg.html).

Khavari, K.A. and Khavari, S.W., 1989, *Creating a Successful Family.* London: Sterling Publishers.

Khinduka, S.K., 1987, Social Work and the Human Services. In *Encyclopedia of Social Work*, Silver Spring: National Association of Social Workers.

Kirk, S.A., 1999, Introduction. In S.A. Kirk (Ed.) *Social Work Research Methods: Building Knowledge for Practice.* New York: NASW Press.

Klein, M.F., 1989, Curriculum Design. In M. Eraut (Ed.) *The International Encyclopaedia of Educational Methodology.* Oxford: Pergamon Press.

Kroehnert, G., 1995, *Basic Training for Trainers: A Handbook for New Trainers.* New York: McGraw Hill Book Co.

Lindsey, D. and Kirk, S.A., 1992, The Role of Social Work Journals in the Development of a Knowledge Base for the Profession, *Social Service Review,* 295-310.

Lions Quest Skills, n.d., *Lions Quest Skills for Adolescence Programme.*

Lowman, J., 1984, *Mastering the Techniques of Teaching*. New Delhi: Prentice Hall of India.

1998, *A Manual for Participatory Training Methods in Development*. New Delhi: Society for Participatory Research in Asia.

Mattaini, M.A., 1995, Knowledge for Practice. In C.H. Meyer and M.A. Mattaini (Eds.) *The Foundations of Social Work Practice: A Graduate Text.* Washington, D.C.: National Association of Social Workers, 59-85.

Morris, L.L. and Fitz-Gibbon, C.T., 1978, *How to Measure Programme Implementation*. London: Sage Publications.

Mullen, E.J., 2002, Evidence-Based Social Work - Theory and Practice: Historical and Reflective Perspective, paper presented at the 4th International Conference on Evaluation for Practice, University of Tampere, Tampere, Finland.

Mumford, A., 2000, *Effective Learning*. Hyderabad: Universities Press.

Nicholson, L.J., 1990, Introduction. In L.J. Nicholson (Ed.) *Feminism/ Postmodernism*. New York: Routledge.

O'Brien, R., 1998, An Overview of the Methodological Approach of Action Research.

Orlosky, D.E. and Smith, B.O., 1978, *Curriculum Development: Issues and Insights*. Chicago: Rand McNally College Publishing Co.

Ornstein, A.C. and Hunkins, F.P., 1998, *Curriculum: Foundations, Principles, and Issues*. Englewood Cliffs, New Jersey: Prentice Hall.

Parsons, R.J., Jorgensen, J.D. and Hernandez, S.H., 1994, *The Integration of Social Work Practice*. Belmont, California: Brooks/ Cole Publishing Company.

Percival, F. and Ellington, H., 1984, *A Handbook of Educational Methodology*. New York: Kogan Page.

Pinderhughes, E., 1995, Direct Practice Overview. In *Encyclopedia of Social Work*. Washington, D.C.: National Association of Social Workers, 740-751.

Powers, G.T., Meenaghan, T.M. and Toomey, B.G., 1985, *Practice focused Research: Integrating Human Service Practice and Research*. New Jersey: Prentice Hall, Inc.

Freire, P., 1972, *Pedagogy of the Oppressed*. London: Penguin Books.

Rajput, J.S., n.d. Towards a Dynamic Evaluation System, (www.ncert.nic.in/icutodyev.htm).

Rees, F., 1998, *The Facilitator Excellence Handbook: Helping People Work Creatively and Productively Together*. San Francisco: Jossey-Bass Pfeiffer.

Rosen, A. and Proctor, E.K., 1979, Specifying the treatment process: The basis for effectiveness research. *Journal of Social Service Research*, 2(1), 25-43.

Rosenau, P.M., 1992, *Post-modernism and the Social Sciences: Insights, Inroads and Intrusions*. Princeton, New Jersey: Princeton University Press.

Ruckdeschel, R.A., 1985, Qualitative Research as a Perspective. *Social Work Research and Abstracts,* 21(2), 17-21.

Smith, B.J. and Delahaye, B.L., 1987, *How to be an Effective Trainer: Skills for Managers and New Trainers*. New York: John Wiley and Sons.

Sohng, S.S.L., 1995, Participatory Research and Community Organizing. A Working Paper presented at The New Social Movement and Community Organizing Conference, University of Washington, Seattle, WA. November 1-3.

Spinks, T. and Clements, P., 1999, *Facilitating Learning: A Sourcebook of Activities.* New Delhi: Viva Books Private Limited.

Staley, J., 1982, *People in Development: A Trainer's Manual for Groups.* Bangalore: SEARCH.

Stroot, S., Keil, V., Stedman, P., Lohr, L., Faust, R., Schincariol-Randall, L., Sullivan, A., Czerniak, G., Kuchcinski, J., Orel, N., and Richter, M., 1998, *Peer Assistance and Review Guidebook.* Columbus, OH: Ohio Department of Education.

Swensen, C.R., 1995, Clinical Social Work. In *Encyclopedia of Social Work.* Washington, D.C.: National Association of Social Workers, 502-513.

Thomas, E.J., 1979, Generating Innovations in Social Work: The Paradigm of Developmental Research. *Journal of Social Service Research,* 2, 95-116.

Toohey, S., 1999, *Designing Courses for Higher Education.* Buckingham: Open University Press.

University Grants Commission, 1980, *Review of Social Work Education in India: Retrospect and Prospect,* New Delhi.

Vijayalakshmi, B., Rao, K.V. and Devi Prasad, B., 1996, Trends in Articles Published in *The Indian Journal of Social Work,* 1971-1990, *The Indian Journal of Social Work,* 56(3), 442-460.

Weick, A., 1994, Reconstructing Social Work Education. In J. Laird (Ed.) *Revisioning Social Work Education: A Social Reconstructionist Approach.* New York: The Haworth Press, 11-30.

Wheeler, D.K., 1967, *Curriculum Process.* London: University of London Press Limited.

World Health Organization, 1999, *Partners in Life Skills Education: Conclusions from a United Nations Inter-Agency Meeting*. Geneva.

Williams, S. Seed, J. and Mwau, A., 1994, *The Oxfam Gender Training Manual.* Oxford: Oxfam.

Index